A WEALTH *of* POSSIBILITIES

A WEALTH
of
POSSIBILITIES

NAVIGATING FAMILY, MONEY, AND LEGACY

Ellen Miley Perry

EGREMONT PRESS

Washington, D.C.

A Wealth of Possibilities by Ellen Miley Perry

Copyright © 2012 Ellen Miley Perry

Chapter illustrations: ©Emmanuel Pierre
Interior cartoons © The New Yorker Collection/www.cartoonbank.com

Egremont Press
info@ellenmperry.com

Designed by Laura Beers

ISBN: 978-0-9883789-0-2

Printed in the United States of America.

10 9 8 7 6 5 4 3

For my parents and siblings;
Bruce Frick Miley,
Joan McCoy Miley,
Michael Miley,
Susan Miley Lee
and for my dear daughter,
Grace

CONTENTS

Introduction

"Family, that dear octopus from whose
tentacles we never quite escape, nor in
our innermost hearts ever quite wish to."
—DOROTHY GLADYS SMITH

I've worked as an advisor to families of substantial financial means for more than twenty years. For the first twelve years, I was primarily a financial advisor to those families. Then, as I found myself drawn more and more into their personal affairs, I gradually shifted focus. I studied Family Systems Theory at the Georgetown Family Center and discovered a new and for me more meaningful calling: helping my clients navigate the unique territory created by the complex combination of family dynamics and substantial wealth.

I've had the privilege of helping some of the country's wealthiest families work to ensure that their family is both resilient and sustainable. I've journeyed with them on their quest to build thriving families. We've pondered together how to keep their vast financial success from negatively impacting specific family members or tearing the family apart. We've sought answers to questions like, How do you keep your feet firmly on the ground in the midst of great abundance? What is the meaning of work in the context of our financial means? How do we move from success to significance? And what is the fundamental purpose of our monetary wealth?

I've seen families through major business transactions, restructurings, and succession to the next generation. I've been there through failed initiatives, marriages, divorces, births, deaths, and illnesses. I've overseen estate planning overhauls, near expatriations, prenuptial agreements, and postnuptial nightmares. I've had a seat at the table through substance abuse, betrayals, interventions, recoveries, and celebrations. The journey has been fascinating and humbling, joyous and tragic.

What I've learned through these experiences is that wealthy families face the same life challenges as all families. Sure, they have ample resources to bolster or even shield them from certain adverse consequences. But I now believe that these protections (some might call them opportunities) come at a very high price. For every "opportunity," wealthy families must also cope with obligation, responsibility, and challenge, not to mention an audience to see them falter or even fail. What's more, their expressions of fear, vulnerability, concern, or regret often fall on deaf or envious ears.

Wealthy families spend much of their time worrying about, planning for, and attending to their finances. They hire and retain teams of experts to help manage their financial wealth. They spend countless days each year attending to money matters, and much time and thought as to how they will pass that wealth on to others.

In the hubbub of all that attentiveness to wealth lies the crux of a fundamental problem, and the reason I felt compelled to write this book. *Few wealthy families devote the same intensity, energy, and commitment to their* human *assets—their family members—as they devote to their* financial *assets.* If a family is to flourish for many generations and wealth is to be a useful means for individuals within the family to self-actualize, attain happiness, and achieve their own successes, devotion to human assets is exactly what's needed most. I use the word "flourish" advisedly to mean something more than personal well-being. In the context of family, individuals flourish if and when they have *1)* a strong sense of individual identity, *2)* well-defined and pursued interests of their own, *3)* the satisfaction of hard work and productivity in life and, perhaps most importantly of all, *4)* a strong connection to other family members.

The challenges I describe in these pages are common to many families, wealthy and not. But I firmly believe that wealth is a magnifier— an accelerator if you will—that can crank everyone and everything up. Kind people can be kinder when they have financial resources, mean people more malevolent, insecure people may become deeply paranoid, and giving people can be tremendously generous. Tensions that occur in virtually all families are intensified when it comes time to allocate or share family assets. Old hurts and relational complexities have ongoing opportunities to be played out around boardroom tables and with shared enterprises, where tangled family emotional complexities can surface and then fester or thrive.

After working with multigenerational families of significant wealth for so many years, I've determined that the most important job of the *second* generation (G2) is to develop human capital with the same energy and intention G1 used to generate financial capital. If a family is to avoid the "shirtsleeves to shirtsleeves in three generations" problem often associated with wealth, the second, third, and even fourth generations must commit to the personal enhancement and enrichment of each and every family member. They must work hard to maintain healthy family relationships, use their financial resources to enhance the life experiences and opportunities of family members, fully integrate spouses into the family, and, above all, develop practices and policies that create healthy connections.

The healthiest multigenerational families I've known have one thing in common: a family member, or group of family members, devoted deeply to the notion of a healthy, connected, committed, and vibrant family. They don't believe that their only job, or even their most important job, is managing the family's financial assets. These leaders acquire training and obtain skills to encourage the robust connectivity of the family in meaningful ways. They imagine a thriving family and then do all in their power to make that dream come true. They apply the same energy and devotion to this dream as entrepreneurs apply to growing financial assets.

There are no silver bullets, however, and the evolution of a family is undeniably complicated. For all the successes and triumphs I will describe in this book, I've met dozens of families who simply can't achieve the essential ingredients for intimacy and commitment. They can't withstand the anxiety, pain, and stresses of life together, and so they pull apart in one way or another.

During my two decades plus of working with the substantially wealthy, I've experienced my own personal growth, family evolution, and life changes. I have an amazing and complex family, and it provides the single most important sustenance in my life. Nothing comes close to the joy and deep satisfaction I get from my husband, daughter, stepchildren, and five step-grandchildren. My parents and siblings had all passed away by the time I was fifty, leaving me particularly mindful of the frail nature of our lives. All too often I see families mired in arguments, minor disagreements, and estrangements, and I deeply wish for them reconciliation. I know well the ways in which these problems arise; my family of origin was as prone as any to relational issues. I do, however, have a perspective of scarcity borne on the back of loss that orients me differently than some who still have their original family members. My professional and personal experience gives me a lens through which I can try to help others think about the conservation of their own families, and the healing and eventual thriving they could enjoy.

I have not developed my insights and perspectives entirely on my own. Over the years, I have been honored to work with many thoughtful and talented professionals from varied disciplines who have taught, inspired, and supported me in so many ways. This book is a compilation of the experiences and wisdom of many family members, advisors to families, and colleagues too numerous to mention by name. You all have added significantly to the store of knowledge presented in this book, and I thank you.

In working with families of wealth, I've witnessed many unusual circumstances, been privy to a wide range of reactions and responses, and learned many valuable life lessons. For practical purposes, I've synthesized my observations and knowledge into five fundamental lessons, which you will recognize as the five chapters of this book:

CONNECT

BE GREAT PARENTS

PITCH A BIG TENT

BECOME EMOTIONALLY FLUENT

CULTIVATE JOY

The chapters are meant to be read in whatever order works for you—start to finish or as the spirit moves you. Feel free to dive in anywhere! I only hope that you will find the thread that resonates with you and leads you to paths and processes that will enable your own family to flourish.

Few wealthy families devote the same intensity, energy, and commitment to their *human* assets—their family members— as they devote to their *financial* assets.

ONE

CONNECT

"Pay attention.
It's all about paying attention.
Attention is vitality.
It connects you with others."
—SUSAN SONTAG

Click. Click. Click. The first sound I'd hear when my father came home from work was the clicking of his shoes across the kitchen linoleum. He'd walk into the den and greet my mother with his usual ebullience. "Hello, Sweetheart" he'd boom. "How are you and where are the girls?" As often as not she'd reply, "I'm fine, Susie is doing her homework upstairs, and Ellen is hiding." Thus began our nightly game of hide-and-seek. I'd hide and Dad would find me by calling out "boop-boop," to which I would echo an often muffled "boop-boop" from whatever complicated, convoluted spot I was twisted into.

I started with the usual places—behind the sofa, under a table or bed, in a closet. But eventually I branched out: the bottom of my parents' clothes hamper (dirty laundry piled on top of me), inside the dryer (spine curved along the inside of the drum), the bottom cabinet of the hall hutch, under the kitchen sink. My sister and mother often had to help with the execution, taking pride in suggesting particularly puzzling locations. The trickier the space the better. Dad would discover me and I'd leap into his arms, squealing with happiness. Years later we'd still laugh about certain antics, like when Susie, before I learned to tell time, would try to hide me hours early just to get me out of her way. Boop-boop was an evening ritual of connection and joy that marked the end of the workday and the beginning of family time. It was a sweet and funny touchstone of connection for our family. We must have played hundreds of times when I was between the ages of five and ten.

This story has a twist, however. When I was ten, my brother Michael, then twenty-one, died in a helicopter crash in Vietnam. My mother received the news just like every other mom during that era, from two uniformed army officers who arrived unannounced to tell her and give her an official letter. Our entire family changed in that moment. My parents coped with our loss by remaining strong and moving ahead. My mother, a good Catholic, held on to the belief that God wouldn't give her something she was unable to handle. But we rarely talked about Mike anymore, and they hid their grief at the bottom of their hearts, invisible to others. The daily small moments of lightness, including boop-boop, were lost to sadness and despair, and I learned to hide in other, more complicated ways. You had to work hard to really know me beyond the external veneer of openness; my deeper self was out of sight, the chance of meaningful connection more remote.

I share this story with you because I believe it illustrates the delight and fragility of connection and the complexity of the human being. *Connection is a paradox: basic and life-affirming and also convoluted by emotional intricacy.* We long to be seen and known deeply, and yet we often protect ourselves from the vulnerability that comes with that kind of intimacy. But connection is the most important foundation on which to build any life, and most certainly the lives of our children. Without it we risk losing the potential for a meaningful life. Many families, like mine, learn the hard way that the threads of connection can be frail and vulnerable. Families who have been financially successful often find that the pressure to succeed, and the very energy and attention that such success demands, present huge challenges to intimacy. When looking at the families who have achieved financial success, people often are puzzled by their struggles with connection and closeness to family. How can something so basic be so hard, particularly when there are so many fewer daily stresses and so much more money and so many more resources to support togetherness? The reason, I've learned, is that meaningful relationships can't happen without meaningful connections.

I believe, as does Edward M. (Ned) Hallowell, M.D., author of *The Childhood Roots of Adult Happiness,* that the children of the very wealthy are at relatively high risk for feeling unconnected or, worse, truly being unconnected.[1] On the one hand, children of the very successful and affluent want for few material possessions, enriching experiences, empowering opportunities; there is little they need that can't be provided. On the other hand, they often long for more emotional connection, starting with availability from their often absent and/or distracted parents.

Hallowell points to the National Longitudinal Study of Adolescent Health as one of the most important, comprehensive, and reliable studies ever undertaken of young people in America. (Although initiated in the late 1990s, the study continues to track participants as they mature, and the results have been confirmed through additional research.) The study surveyed 90,000 young people, age twelve to sixteen, in 145 schools across America about their lives, education, peers, parents and family life, risk behaviors, hopes and dreams for the future, health, and sense of self-esteem—more than a hundred variables in the students' lives were addressed. Among the core findings are that children could be protected from negative outcomes in life by being connected at home and being connected at school.

Connectedness, for this study, was defined as "closeness to mother and/or father, perceived caring by mother and/or father, satisfaction with the relationship with mother and/or father, and feeling understood, loved, wanted, and paid attention to by family members."[2]

In this chapter we will explore the most effective ways to connect with your family:

- Communication
- Trust Building
- Family Meetings and Mission Statements

Wealth owners and inheritors—people whose lives are full of work-related responsibilities, major obligations, and personal commitments—need exceptional intentionality and discipline in order to connect with and nurture the people they love most. The greatest tool, if only they can learn how to use it, is communication. The trust resulting from strong communication skills will profoundly impact their family's sustainability.

Communication

Families who have strong and healthy communication skills can weather significant challenges and remain intact. Those with limited effective communication skills are vulnerable to the challenges of life pulling them apart.

Families who flourish are those who master the art of having difficult conversations. They learn how to communicate about what matters most and become adept at bringing their most productive behaviors to conversations with family members. Their members learn to identify what kinds of conversations, or which family members, are the most challenging for them, and work hard to improve those relationships. Above all, they learn to listen.

A common and complicating factor for G2 and G3 is that inheritors hardly ever learn fabulous communication skills from their parents. Why? Because highly successful entrepreneurs are often poor listeners. They are rarely patient, curious about the other's perspective, or sensitive about ensuring that the other person feels heard. (Should I say this more gently, dear reader?) Successful entrepreneurs are used to being heard and, when in dialogue, they are controlling by nature, dynamic, and fast-paced rather than patient. They rarely spend much time seeking information about why and how their children see things differently. They'd rather work harder to "correct" their children's thinking!

Instead of communicating, such wealth owners often believe that if they can just do a better job of describing the situation, their kids will agree with them. They think it's a failed communication (which it is!), a lack of understanding on their kids' part, rather than a substantive difference of opinion at play. They don't tend to remain curious about the other's position for long, and they risk family members shutting down, moving emotionally or physically away, or putting up strong boundaries—none of which contributes to a healthy, flourishing family.

Further complicating effective communication among family members is the fact that the successful and wealthy often find it difficult to be emotionally vulnerable. They are afraid to show their weaknesses, risk disappointment, or potentially invite betrayal and deceit. They often learn to protect themselves from others, to keep their thoughts to themselves, to remain private and discreet about the complications of their lives. What can begin as good manners ("We don't talk about our good fortune") can bleed into full relational distancing and the

buildup of barriers. *To earn trust, one must be vulnerable. It is the only path to real intimacy.*

But intimacy can be challenging for the wealthy. I've worked with many families who feel that they're easy targets for requests, needs, and envy. They worry that others, even those who appear to be sincere, in the end only want something—a donation, a job, a reference or access to a third party, investment opportunities or a loan, or perhaps just the chance to be part of their seemingly lovelier lives. Once this fear has been realized a few times, it's quite natural to develop trust issues. Opening up becomes virtually impossible; it's much safer to stick with suspicious and distrustful feelings. These "easy targets" may feel that they must remain vigilant against the threat of being used. They are overly self-protective because they worry that others don't truly like or love them for themselves. They teach their children by example to be equally distrustful, and that becomes an unintended legacy.

A LIGHTHEARTED APPROACH

One of my clients (I'll call him Robert) is a giant in every sense. Big, robust, dominant, Robert is a beacon of intelligence, success, and generosity in his town, his state, even in the world. Countless people look up to him, and many, *many*, seek a connection. He was raised in the humblest of homes, one of several children, and has risen to accomplish an astounding amount financially, philanthropically, socially, and creatively. Robert has not lost his humanity nor his compassion in the process, and yet he was inspired to have new business cards printed after the billion-dollar sale of his company, cards that simply state his name and the words "Thank you for not asking me for anything." He often jokes about the cards, but then quickly explains that he feels others often look to him to provide solutions to their personal problems. He didn't print these cards because he's insensitive, uncaring, or stingy. Quite the contrary! He did it because he felt targeted at times, and he saw a way to preempt the "ask."

Unlike other wealth owners I've known, Robert remains good-humored and generally available to many. He has a vital, expansive, philanthropic life, but rarely feels used. Many wealth owners have just learned to deal with the discomfort that comes from having so much more than most. They find ways to say no gracefully, to do what they can for the people and causes that are meaningful to them and to refuse those that aren't. They learn not to feel used by those who want something from them. They see their good fortune, at its core, as security.

I've known others, however, who have had very different reactions to their wealth. The financial resources they have result in detachment and separation from others. For every "Robert," I have many, particularly inheritors, who harbor fear and distrust. If we dig just below the guarded surface of these individuals, we often find people afraid of being hurt, afraid of being abandoned, afraid of being rejected. The eldest generations must avoid bestowing suspicion and fear upon their children, for these are all barriers to communication, trust, and the meaningful human connection that flows from letting others in.

Robert and his wife worked hard to raise children who are open and largely available to connection and vulnerability. Not that it was always natural and easy, but Robert's own modeling of these characteristics and their devotion to family allowed for that

> possibility in the next generation. And their children
> have devoted themselves to personal growth and
> enjoy a rich connectedness. They meet regularly,
> have twice-annual retreats, work hard on the rela-
> tionships within their generation, and appreciate
> the importance of connection to the ultimate health
> and sustainability of their family.

Trust

We often observe aloofness in the children of the wealthy—a cool
remoteness that seems at times to be superiority, but often masks
a fear of being hurt or rejected. To protect their children from risk
and potential hurt, wealthy parents often model behavior that unintentionally teaches their children to distrust others. It often begins
with keeping secrets. Elementary school kids are tutored in discretion. Their parents tell them, "We don't talk about our good fortune,
vacations, family gatherings, money, plane, Grandpa's business, etc."

I'm not suggesting that teaching discretion is always wrong, but I am
suggesting that it has an unintended consequence. Children who are
taught to withhold personal information get the very clear message
that others are not to be trusted with important facts about their lives,
and that they must carefully choose what to share. Ultimately, the
children ascertain that other people are not trustworthy. And if the
secrecy isn't explained thoroughly again and again and illustrated well
by the parents—a tall order!—they might misinterpret it as brought
on by embarrassment or shame.

A nuanced and additional complexity is that often the second and
third generations are encouraged to talk openly with only one set of
relatives, the wealthy side. They learn that only certain cousins are
okay to be open with. This creates an unhealthy favoring of one side of

the family and a diminishment of the other. And it isn't just children who are put in this uncomfortable position. Very often spouses feel they can't share the details of their affluent lives—from the extent of the family wealth to the kinds of meetings they attend—with their own parents and siblings!

I've seen such "rules" around communication lead to feelings of disconnection and loneliness for spouses of the wealthy. Again, fear of betrayal and a need for privacy lead the family to insist on secrecy, even when dealing with their in-laws. The spouse is often embarrassed or afraid of being judged. The result is an unhealthy and disconnecting family dynamic, not a spirit of open and trusting communication.

Families who flourish, in contrast, cultivate strong communication skills. They understand the important role that open, frequent, and honest communication plays in the life of their family. They're willing to talk with their children and grandchildren about a wide variety of issues and to learn or hone their communication skills. They listen. And listen. And listen.

Listening well and communicating effectively are critical to meaningful human connectivity because they evidence mutual respect—a precursor to trust. Below are two key tools for improving communication skills and building trust:

1 - Look inward before looking outward.

Barriers to communication are typically established in the early years. Consider your own communications upbringing and then see if that can help you think more clearly about the kind of communication you'd like to establish with family members. Take a moment to reflect on the following:

- Do you and your spouse share attitudes about many important parts of your life, including money?

- What are your concerns about communicating with your siblings, spouses, or children about money issues?

- What is your personal experience with secrets? With embarrassment or betrayal? How has it influenced your behavior?

- How did your parents communicate with you when you were a child? Were they open and receptive to meaningful discussions? What were uncomfortable topics? Did they disagree with one another well? With you?

- What were the messages you received? Were they consistent with your parents' actions? What was missing from the conversation?

2 - Consider a framework to tackle difficult conversations.

The answers to the above questions might help you sort out how to handle tricky issues or conversations with family members. Far too many families simply hope conflicts or challenges will resolve themselves or go away. Clearly, that's not a process that works over time. As anyone who's been married for long knows, a touchy topic that goes ignored is destined to resurface later—and in bigger and more complicated ways. Consider instead approaching such a conversation in this way:

- Identify the issues.

- Ascertain the underlying attitudes and values—yours, your siblings', your spouse's, and your children's. Look at your own attitudes and consider why the other(s) might see things differently.

- Develop a plan, taking into consideration age appropriateness, for what you want to communicate, how you want to say it, and topics that are off-limits.

- Identify opportunities for learning (for now and for later).

- Identify risks inherent in the various scenarios and have a plan for handling difficult situations.

- Consider what is most important in this conversation. Building the relationship? Converting their thinking? An outcome? Being right? Listen, listen, listen.

Conversation frameworks, or plans, for specific situations are all well and good, but there will also be times when you'll be caught completely off guard, like when your child asks, "How much money do you make?" Gulp. Here's how to handle being blindsided:

- If your child (or any family member) initiates a conversation before you've had time to think about what you want to say, respond with something like: "That's a really important question that deserves a thoughtful answer, so I'd like some time to think about it and then come back to you." Then set a time when you will be ready to discuss it.

- If your child asks a question you don't want to answer directly, reply with a question that explores feelings or beliefs/attitudes. "You seem upset about this. Is there something on your mind that we can talk about?"

Family Meetings

For financially successful families with joint enterprises, assets, and philanthropic interests, finding a forum to maintain and enhance their personal connection to one another is important: which brings us to "the family meeting." Family meetings can be a dynamic means of building relationships, establishing connections, and continuing dialogue among family members that promotes more effective communication and trust.

Family meetings are best when held regularly—at least twice annually. They should be open to all adult family members, including spouses. An agenda must be developed in advance, with input from all participants. A skilled facilitator, one who has identified ahead of time any hidden or percolating issues that might surface, should be brought in to run the meeting.

It's important to give the family meeting a tone of professionalism and transparency. Everyone invited should be able to understand in

Arnie Levin

advance what's on the agenda, the purpose and goals of the meeting, how the meeting will be conducted, and what the experience will be like. Many may have quite a bit at stake in these meetings—both emotionally and financially. The less left to chance and happenstance, the more secure everyone will feel.

Agenda items can vary widely. Families might discuss developing leadership in the next generation, financial results, investment opportunities, operating business updates, communication and trust building, estate plans, the selection and performance of money managers, legal issues, use of vacation homes and aircraft, family vacation or reunion plans, and family genealogy, among other issues. Families who meet regularly often develop a template or rhythm that guides the development of each meeting agenda.

When many members of a family come together, the chances increase for intense emotions to surface. We'll discuss this more in subsequent chapters, but insofar as it pertains to the family meeting, here are a few practical actions I've found helpful in keeping difficulties at bay:

- Have the meeting in a "neutral" location—not in the home of a family member or at the office. It keeps the potential dynamics simpler.

- Hold the meeting in a room with good natural light and windows. This allows for better energy for the participants. Trust me on this, it makes a difference.

- Allow for frequent breaks—at least fifteen minutes every two hours. Remember, family relationships can rile anxiety; giving participants breaks makes for a more productive meeting.

- The elders, trusts, or family office should foot all travel and related expenses. Don't nickel-and-dime participants over sodas they took from the minibar or the in-room movie they watched after the meeting. If you want willing and vital participation, make it easy and comfortable for all involved. Pay for the plane, train, hotel, car, gas, tolls, babysitters, meals, cabs, tips—*all of it*. It will be money well spent.

The underlying goal of my suggestions is to create a welcoming space, both physically and emotionally, for every family member. The long-term purpose of these meetings is to create and sustain strong family connections. Everything you do and plan for the meeting should move you closer toward that. If you find yourself considering something that would work against closer family bonds (such as leaving out spouses, holding a secret pre-meeting caucus, insisting that everyone pay their own transportation), consider that a red flag in your planning process. Family meetings can be useful arenas for spirited discussions, even debates, but they should never turn into battlefields. That said, some conflicts can't be avoided; do what you can to minimize those within your control.

For many families, beginning the process of family meetings can be easier and less complex than those described here for larger families. A short weekly meeting during dinner with your children can be a great time to discuss upcoming family events, holidays, household responsibilities and chores, school events and family updates. Each person can take a turn discussing what's on their mind. Some families add rituals such as the lighting of a candle or the singing of a song.

A colleague of mine described her family meetings in which she, her husband, and their teenage daughters hold a 30-minute Sunday evening meeting while their younger daughter colors on the floor. They follow this with the distribution of allowances and ice cream sundaes—calling the meetings Sunday Sundaes.

The Role of the Facilitator

Having an experienced, *non-family* member organize and facilitate is vital to ensuring a productive meeting. Ideally, hire someone not currently affiliated with your family, but if that's not feasible, choose your talented and skilled attorney, or the CEO of your family business.

Under no circumstances allow a family member to run the meeting. Think of it this way: orchestra conductors don't try to play an instrument while they lead. Facilitators, like conductors, should be mindful of bigger strategies, desired outcomes, potentially complicated issues, and possible relational complexities. They should have talked to all participants in advance of the meeting and understand well how to navigate the group forward. They hold the responsibility of keeping the space safe for all and for dealing with complex issues should they arise. They don't have a dog in the fight, so they're completely unbiased and, more important, nonjudgmental.

Facilitators are compensated either by the day, year, or by the project. A strong facilitator will have formal training, references, and long-standing clients with whom you can speak. They should not be compensated in any way other than by you, meaning no third-party payments from your investment advisor or trust company.

Ideally, facilitators become intimate members of the business/family/ enterprise circle—not a one-time resource brought in to help with one or two meetings. They should learn the patterns of your family and become a deeply important resource for all generations. If you choose someone already involved with your family, such as your lawyer or CEO, be sure they have strong facilitation skills! Err on the side of skills and experience rather than intimate, existing knowledge of your family or enterprise. Understand that this person must be seen by all members of your family as unbiased and fair. (This is more challenging if you use an employee or confidant of one family member.)

The best facilitators aren't just able to run a good meeting. They're also leaders, who will raise topics they see can enhance your family's ability to thrive. They will anticipate what's around the next corner for your family and can help you get through it. They will ask the hard questions you can't ask yourselves. They will speak truthfully and openly, without fear of retribution. They are willing to be fired or, if the relationship is not working out, they will tell you when it's time for them to step aside.

Family Mission Statements

Another way to build connection in families of wealth is by coming up with a family mission statement that describes the values and purpose of the family's collective life. This document is, in essence, communication immemorial. Developing a mission statement is a potentially wonderful means of establishing clarity and encouraging unity among family members. What many don't realize, however, is that the process by which it is created is as important to connection as the statement of purpose that emerges. Keep the following in mind when looking to create your family's mission statement:

- **Hold a series of special meetings.** Take time to discuss the "big picture." What do we represent as a family and what is the purpose of our resources? Give each question the appropriate amount of thought and discussion.

- **Hire a skilled facilitator to assist you.** As with family meetings, a facilitator, whether a trusted colleague or a consultant, can be invaluable in an important discussion such as this—better yet if you can find one who has been through this before. Consider bringing in someone to organize and then move the discussion forward, leaving interested family members to voice their thoughts and concerns without having to worry about the specifics of the ultimate product.

- **Take your time.** A year or two—more, if necessary. Remember, most families function without a mission statement. Allow ample time (and space) for the mission that resonates best with your family to emerge in the family consciousness.

- **Don't try to write the statement all at once.** It often makes sense to let the spirit of the mission statement percolate at your family meetings, then assign a point person to draft a statement for review. While some families could conceivably knock out a dynamite mission statement in an afternoon, most find themselves haggling over words. Better to sort this out over a series of meetings, and with a facilitator.

• **Look to the family dynamic.** Anticipate how your family works together. Who dominates discussions, who quietly has good ideas, who gains consensus well, who causes conflict, and who is passive in the moment and then derails the process later? Understand the patterns that exist and try to address them through the process.

• **Get everyone involved.** While only a few people—maybe even only one—should be involved in the actual drafting, the discussion should involve as many family members as possible, to increase the chances that the mission will resonate with the most family members.

• **Reflect as much as possible the common interests of the family.** If the mission statement represents only the most senior, vocal, or passionate members, only the most senior, vocal, and passionate will be prepared to work toward it.

• **Be as specific as possible.** It's much easier to broaden a mission later to welcome new family member interests than it is to narrow one's mission and ditch a cherished element.

• **Have fun.** As much as you can, cultivate a spirit of lightness and curiosity around this activity.

• **Don't forget about it.** The mission statement can be a unifying and energizing force for your family. It can be a valuable compass if you're willing to let it lead you, so try to find ways to use it often. Refer to it during times of transition; open family meetings with a recitation of it; have it printed on business cards that you give to every family member. (This last goal also serves to keep it short.)

Whether via a family meeting or a mission statement or some other process for facilitating constructive communication, what you're doing in all these efforts is creating a foundation—nurturing connection—to help support family members as they navigate complex relationships over many years. A patriarch and matriarch can often provide the kind of overarching thematic guidance that permeates a family and helps all members to see themselves both as individuals and as a collective whole. But as G2 and G3 move into adulthood, it becomes more difficult for any one individual to lead the family system. Family meetings and mission statements can help subsequent generations maintain their focus and cohesion.

To flourish, the family must nurture and grow human capital with the same passion that the original wealth creator put toward building financial capital. Nothing will contribute more to the resilience and connectedness of the family. Connection means being available to your family in meaningful, constant ways. It means doing the hard work of being a great communicator and developing processes and means to hear and honor individual voices. It means building mutual respect and trust. Family meetings, rituals, and mission statements encourage connection. This process of connection is a life-long devotion. It is the bedrock upon which all other practices are rooted and without which your family will not flourish. It is the beginning and the end, the simplest and the most profound. Within meaningful and sustainable connection lies all possibility.

Vulnerability is the only real path
to intimacy and connection.

"Children are the living messages
we send to a time we will not see."
—NEIL POSTMAN

Intentional parenting is a lifetime opportunity. This means imagining and then realizing strong parenting skills, wherever you are on the family tree. It's never too late to be a better parent, but the earlier we learn the principles of strong parenting the higher the chances our children have of being successful parents themselves. *When I cut to the chase, through all of my strategies and counsel, I find one over-arching truth: the secret to a thriving, connected family is focused, intentional parenting.*

What follows in this chapter are not my thoughts on the vast domain of good parenting skills and practices. What I'm offering are reflections on the unique challenges, complications, and opportunities of child-rearing in the context of privilege and wealth. These issues require particular attention to and heightened awareness of psychological and emotional nuances.

For the wealthy family who maintains family cohesion through shared responsibilities and enterprises, parenting styles and principles apply throughout the lives of both the parents and the children, regardless of age, gender, or their roles within the family. It's critical, therefore, to try to get it right as early on as possible.

The Basics

Time and consistency are strongholds of a rock-solid parenting foundation. "The key to being a good parent is wanting to be a good parent strongly enough to make the time to do it," says Dr. Ned Hallowell.[3] This can be especially tricky for the wealthy, who have the option of subcontracting some of their parenting obligations. What exactly is the right amount of time? What's a healthy trade-off between time with family and time for career and interests? What pieces of the vast array of parental duties can be handed off to household help without detriment to the children? How much do children really need parents on a day-to-day basis?

Child psychologists agree that there really is no substitute for consistent parental love. Consistency forms the basis of a child's sense of security and identity in life, and contributes mightily to their sense of confidence. Consistency also prepares them for healthy adult relationships. Its absence places them on shaky emotional ground and creates difficulty in many other kinds of attachments in life.

The damage and heartbreak I often see in second and third generations is a result of a somewhat intangible sort of deprivation of parental attention and attachment. It's not always easy to spot and harder yet to pinpoint exactly what isn't working. These seemingly involved parents are often actually quite distracted from their children. To complicate matters, their parenting sometimes presents as overattentiveness of the wrong kind, as in what Robert Kegan describes as "parents who expect more of a child than the child can possibly deliver."

*I think we could conclude that our culture deserves high marks
when it comes to providing adolescents with a continuous experience of challenge. . . . [However,] the experience of challenge without support is painful. . . . These disappointing adolescents may be
in over their heads, and their situation is all the more dangerous for
being misunderstood by those adults whose expectations they are
disappointing. We all feel much less sympathetic toward people
we think have let us down because they choose to than toward
people who let us down because they are unable to do otherwise.*[4]

Kegan goes on to explain that being in over their heads is not necessarily a bad thing if they also have the experience of effective support.
Such supports constitute a "holding environment" that provides both
welcoming acknowledgment to exactly who the person is right now
as he or she is, and foster their evolution.

The wealthy and successful often have mastered providing a challenging environment for their children, but have not always mastered the
effective support and holding environment Kegan describes.

Here's another dynamic I see time and again: parents who have themselves accomplished much and now expect more from their children
than is healthy or natural. They seem to parent each child in an aspi-
rational way, making decisions and propelling their kids forward in
ways that speak more to their dreams for their kids than to the reality
of their child's capabilities. Some have created businesses and are now
seeking leadership from the next generation. They're looking for a
child, niece, or nephew who is like them—driven, accomplished,
devoted, and dynamic. And guess what. They're often disappointed.
The powerful internal engine that fuels entrepreneurs isn't heredi-
tary. The complex combination of character traits, fears, dreams, and
needs don't pass naturally down through the generations, nor does

one successful generation necessarily beget another. Quite the contrary, in fact. Despite that truth, we seem to have reached a point in which expecting—even demanding—the extraordinary from our kids is perceived as a badge of great parenting.

Some affluent families are stymied in parenting by the very traits that make them so successful in business. The singular focus, hard work, even obsession that great financial success requires leaves limited time for life balance and parenting. And while wealthy parents rarely have the compulsory work pressures of people of modest means—the need to keep a job to feed the family or pay the rent—they do have work pressures that drive their careers and energize their successful businesses. It's rare to see a highly successful businessperson who values and boldly demonstrates life balance. The pulls and tugs of enterprise—from operating roles to board positions to committee responsibilities and philanthropic commitments—can detract from the work of raising their own families.

How then do parents raise their children well while still pursuing their own professional dreams? They need to be willing to compromise in ways that they didn't have to prior to having children. Even more, they need to be willing to admit that they simply can't "have it all."

To be a great parent in the midst of your highly successful and demanding financial reality, you need to:

- Tame the machinery
- Be intentional in your parenting
- Teach your children financial literacy
- Shrink the "Big Shadow"

Tame the Machinery

The wealth and abundance that families who have been financially successful acquire has a sort of centrifugal force that swirls with energy and demands attention. The enterprise issues are often complex, the businesses robust, and the teams of advisors and employees vast. The people and businesses surrounding such enterprises create a "machinery" that meets the needs of the owners. Teams, divisions, subsidiaries, and staffs—from administrative and accounting to legal and strategic—identify, investigate, and implement the widespread and often complex tasks required by these financial families.

This complexity can overwhelm children; worse, it can make them feel insignificant or unimportant in the face of it all. Even accomplished adult children can feel diminished by the sheer power and scope of the enterprises. Complex business strategies, high-powered boards of directors, and global companies can all distance second and third generations from first-generation leaders. At its worst, this disconnect can lead to full-on estrangement. The dynamic leaders of those businesses are often intellectual powerhouses, meeting with and collaborating with phenomenal minds daily. Their ideas are big, their connections astounding. Children, even those grown, can shrink by their own estimation.

A young woman I know describes this scenario perfectly. "My father can't accept the smallness of my dreams; he needs to constantly find ways to enhance and expand what I'm doing. My business can't just be local and contained; it needs to be dynamic and global and highly profitable for him to be interested in it. I avoid talking to him about it because I'm constantly justifying my plans and resisting his suggestions of ways to improve and expand it. And each time I do speak to him, and I do justify my plans, I come away feeling that he's disappointed in me for my seeming lack of vision or passion."

It's possible that she's right, that he is longing for her to have dreams that are bigger and more compelling, both conceptually and financially. But it could be that he's actually proud and interested in her work, and relates to it through both his own experiences and the grandness with which entrepreneurs move through life, but that she "hears" and then filters his comments though her own sense of inadequacy.

Be Intentional in Your Parenting

Parenting brings out the best and the worst in every person. Most parents experience love that transcends understanding and at the same time most of us have been brought to our knees in difficult parenting times. I can list for you each and every one of my bad parenting moments, and I can easily recall the shame I've felt when I've over-reacted, overpenalized, or underappreciated my daughter. I'm sure most parents can relate. The truth that has emerged, for me and my clients, is that parenting is most successful when one is intentional about one's objectives.

The clearer we are about the characteristics we hope to see in our children, the culture and environment in our home, the priorities we emphasize, and the trade-offs we're willing to make, the more satisfied we are with our parenting.

Parenting requires that the parent be both a sprinter and a marathoner; a strategist and a tactician; a calm voice; and a firm, and consistent, enforcer—for decades! I've had many discussions with clients and friends who feel there are times that are more important for parenting. Many contend that the really important time to be more present is when the children are teens. Others feel the critical time is when they're quite young. The truth is, we're all trying to find a formula to help us do the impossible—balance our own needs with our kids' needs. As a working mother of an elementary school daughter, I run this calculation in my head each time I take on a new client or agree to a new project or board role. We have some fictitious calculus in our heads that's all our own, and that guides and validates our decisions.

One thing that wealth adds to the parental equation is the privilege of choice and the element of distraction. Outsourcing tasks related to child care liberates wealthy parents for work, travel, philanthropy, pleasure, and hobbies. The ability to afford the highest-quality child care is an important differentiator. Affluent parents can find and retain nannies, babysitters, and tutors with advanced degrees and impressive work experience. We can rest assured that our children are in safe, competent, and reliable hands when we're not with them. We're fooling ourselves, however, if we think child care—even the best child care—can totally replicate consistent, healthy attention from a parent. *There's absolutely no fully comparable substitute for time with your children.*

BREATHING ROOM

As you can probably tell, I struggle with balancing time for work with time for my daughter— how much of each is enough? Most recently I saw what a difference it made to our daughter when I took a sabbatical to write. We moved to our country house in New England for two years so I could focus on this book, a complex choice given that my husband, Rob, works in D.C. and has a grown daughter and three granddaughters there. Further, I have dear friends there, a close relationship with my stepdaughter, and, more practically, benefit from easy access to major airports for traveling to see my clients.

We feel a strong sense of community in D.C.; we love where we live and have meaningful connections to our neighbors. But the three years prior to our move were fraught with loss and grief. My darling father died at eighty-nine, and a year later my sister Susie died after a long and terrible fight with cancer. During this time we also lost a very good friend and both of our old dogs. We were reeling.

This book had been brewing in me for years. My family, friends, and colleagues teased that they'd grown weary of hearing me talk about it. But I couldn't summon the energy to get started— couldn't find creative space within my grief to organize and execute. Then Rob suggested we move to the country for a bit so I could write and he could slow down from his hectic travel schedule.

What happened when we uprooted ended up being about more than having the space and a place to write; it became the means to finding the space and time for our family to heal and reconnect. In D.C. we lived by our calendars and performed a weekly pas de deux of scheduling. In the country we slowed down and time literally expanded. We read and walked, cooked and talked, watched the seasons change. We gardened, dealt with snowdrifts and dead batteries, caught a wild chipmunk in the house, and played hundreds of games of Crazy Eights. Our family began to thrive again and I rediscovered my spirit and the book started to flow. We gained new sensibilities about how pace and time impact each other. I learned many lessons about parenting and the importance of the basic ways of being present with and for our daughter. I was less hurried, and therefore hurried Grace less, and that has had an impact. Like others, perhaps, I am very differently paced from my daughter. I move faster and am more comfortable with quick changes and hasty transitions. Grace is calmer, more deliberate; she prefers slower, anticipated changes, routine, predictability. I hadn't appreciated the cost on both of us, of this difference. During our sabbatical, I slowed down a good bit, but perhaps more than anything I took the time to talk to her about upcoming changes and transitions rather than foisting them on her. And she thrived in that combination of a slightly slower pace paired with more discussion about our schedule.

What busy, ambitious parents often fail to understand—what I have failed at times to understand—is the unintended consequence of being diverted from our children over long periods of time. True, children from all socioeconomic backgrounds have to cope with the issue of absent parents. But the difference is that the children of the very wealthy often perceive that their parents are choosing to be away from them for something better, whereas the children of the poor and middle class more typically feel that their parents are only trying to take care of them by working hard to get ahead.

Parents who are absent and/or distracted unintentionally send the very clear message to their children that being important and successful—winning awards, traveling the globe—matters most to them. The fact that Mom and Dad aren't home on any given Tuesday night helping with homework or a school project sends a powerful and undeniable signal. Do you need to be home every single night? NO! Of course not! Do you need to hover about tending to their every need? NO! But should you have dinner with them five nights a week? Yes, I believe so. And should you make it to most of their sports events, school plays, and field trips? Yes, yes, yes.

First-rate educations, enriching opportunities, and excellent child care are important, but in no way are they more important than spending time with you. Simply being with your kids—on good days and lousy days—is critical. Being absent (or being with them physically but being electronically distracted) makes your priorities painfully clear to them.

I'm not saying parents shouldn't have important careers and professional lives. Having a fulfilling professional life of your own teaches your children other essential lessons about passion and dedication and meaning. What's damaging to children is the degree to which parents become so totally absorbed in work that they have little energy, creativity, or time for them. Measuring one's own level of distraction versus attentiveness is that much harder if you believe you've gone to great lengths to organize interesting activities and competent child care for your children. It's so much easier to rationalize your time away from them when they are having wonderful opportunities.

I know one family who rationalizes time spent away from children every day. The parents are remarkably accomplished. Both the mother and the father run companies within the large family conglomerate, and the companies are multinational in scope and carry numerous product lines. Both parents are devoted to the family legacy and the financial success of their companies. They're following in the footsteps of a larger-than-life patriarch beloved by his community and constituents. His daughter and her husband are trying mightily to create additional wealth and success and prestige for the family. The mother leaves the house at 4:30 A.M. to exercise before work and rarely returns home before 9 P.M. The father travels extensively to Asia and South America—very often gone for a week at a time.

"*Your daughter called—you promised to play phone tag with her today.*"

Their four daughters, ranging in age from elementary to middle school, are all bright and energetic and involved in a variety of school and after-school activities. They rely heavily on two nannies and a housekeeper. Both nannies have advanced degrees in education and are delightful and impressive in many ways. They provide consistency and connectedness that the children need, and all of the children are successful in school.

What these children don't have is a deeply profound connection to their parents. The nannies spend virtually all of their waking hours with them, attending most activities and sporting events with them. Their parents come when they can, but their attendance is sporadic at best. It's the nannies who are there in good and bad, ups and downs. The parents are able to grasp the broad-brush strokes of their lives—the big issues, the great victories, and "epic" (that's the preteen talking) failures. But it's the nannies who understand the microfibers of their days.

When I once suggested we gather the family—parents and children—for a Monday dinner, I saw right away that the day-to-day connection of mealtime was missing. My goal was to bring the children in on the idea of regularly gathering as a family and discussing family goals and priorities. When we sat down to dinner, I was astounded to see how surprised and unsettled the children were. They didn't seem to know what to do with the reality that their parents were home with them at 6 P.M., sitting around the table, trying to have a family discussion. They looked to their nannies for guidance throughout the meal. This is an extreme example, but it raises a fundamental theme: be available to your kids even in the face of a busy career. *Manage your time and your ambition in ways that leave room for your children to feel very important to you and to be very important to you.*

Teach Your Children Financial Literacy

Successful families often ask me to help them design and implement a training program of sorts for upcoming generations, a means to educate their children on everything from finance and business to navigating relationships in which only one person has wealth, to philanthropy and discovering their own passions.

Many parents I meet with are the wealth creators themselves, not the inheritors. They know how to succeed in business but are less clear on how to deal with the often confusing and overwhelming "human" issues that come with the wealth. Further, the challenges their children will face are foreign to them. Finally, as if that isn't enough, first-generation wealth creators are often inclined to make the lives of their children easier through their financial resources. They've worked so hard to attain freedom and security that they, quite naturally, wish to create more ease in the lives of their children. These parents are often seeking ways to help their children figure out a world that they themselves had to learn about the hard way.

While I'm happy to help strategize and provide guidance and assistance—ideally complementing what the parents are already doing—ultimately it's the parents' job to teach their children lessons around managing and living with wealth. A twice-annual meeting with an advisor can't begin to address the complex issues these young people face.

Instead, the idea of financial competence should be an ongoing and integrated part of the family fabric, much like good manners, morals, tolerance, and flexibility. Parents who make transparent the expenses of running a family life, vacations, and clothes give their children skills they will use their entire lives. Intertwining such lessons into dinner conversations, grocery store outings, vacation travels, and before any major family purchase keeps the discussion relevant and open.

The issue of teaching money management brings up another irrefutable difference between the affluent and the middle class: less financially advantaged families typically have a *lot* of discussion about money—how they will afford schools, trips, cars—and those children often see in real time how the parents set priorities, make choices, and delay gratification based on reality. These lessons become part of the kids' everyday lives—no special teachers required, no consultants with preplanned lessons. These children live money management, all day every day. Many wealthy families, in contrast, struggle to draw a line between overindulgence and opportunity. With no—or certainly fewer—externally imposed financial limits, when is it appropriate to create them?

INDULGENCE OR OPPORTUNITY?

"Please, Daddy," Caroline implores as they get in line at the bookstore, arms laden with books. "I've enough money left on the gift card to get all these, may I please get them?" Caroline's father and mother are former clients of mine whose two daughters absolutely love to read. Each trip to the bookstore is an opportunity for stoking that passion for books, exploring and developing greater learning. But where are the limits? How many books is too many? It's hard to blame them for indulging the girls to build robust personal libraries, but when is there too much indulgence, too much abundance?

A love of reading hardly seems a vice worthy of concern. But if Caroline's parents allow excess in books, they lose the chance to teach and develop important skills such as delayed gratification, an ability to discern among various choices, and self-moderation, all of which are deeply important life lessons. Thankfully, Caroline's parents do, in fact, set limits, they teach moderation and delayed gratification as well as financial management. Both daughters get a bookstore "credit card" at the beginning of each quarter worth $50, and both have told me they have learned over time to pace their spending, and that leaving a balance allows them at least one, if not two, more bookstore outings. It teaches personal discipline, wise shopping, and careful planning. Can the parents afford as many books as the girls want? Sure. But how much better to teach them these vital lessons.

Training Wheels

Teaching financial responsibility and literacy to one's children is important for everyone—not just the wealthy. But consider this: if you expect your children to manage some wealth one day, spend time and energy now to ensure they gain the skills needed. You'd never hand your car keys to a child without extensive driving lessons and experience; why would you hand over your wealth? The challenge is that money, at least in the abstract, is often far less interesting to kids than a car!

How *do* you entice them, invite them, and excite them to learn about money? I suggest starting early with an allowance. Think of it as a training tool. Increase the amount each year and give them more responsibility for purchasing their own things—toys when they're young, clothes, iTunes, movies, etc., as they grow older—and truly give them the power, don't overcontrol them.

You can also help them learn about the economic structure of things they're already interested in. If your daughter loves cooking, help her examine a catering business to teach her financial principles in a setting that interests her. If your son or daughter is a sports fan, dissect their favorite team's financial situation. Analyze what they paid for players, total number of tickets likely sold, merchandise—anything that involves money is fair game. Seize on what they love and look at it financially. Next time you go to a restaurant, think and talk with them about all the costs that go into running that business—from food, rent, and labor to advertising and licensing. Help them see it deeply and appreciate it differently.

Finally, painful as it may be, let your children make mistakes with money. Watch them—no judgment!—use up their allowance on something frivolous that makes them then run short on funds and have to do without something they really want. Don't bail them out! You lose the "teachable moment" if there isn't a real consequence to their overspending. It's so much better for them to learn this lesson when the dollar amounts are still small. One family I know has each of their three girls—ages thirteen to eighteen—manage their entire allowance for a four-month period on their own. They buy clothes, books, entertainment, gifts. Their parents pay them in September, in January, and in June. After making mistakes in their early years, the girls became frugal, thoughtful, and careful. The eldest now takes better care of her clothes because she can then sell them to her younger sister when she outgrows them, as can that sister to the youngest one. They've become comparison shoppers, looking for sales and deals, whereas before this process began, they had virtually endless lists of "wants" for their parents to buy.

BOOK BAG

If you have school-age children, run (don't walk!) out and buy Joline Godfrey's *Raising Financially Fit Kids*, a sensational guide to practical, doable, and essential financial training for your kids. It's fun and engaging and full of activities and lessons you can do with your kids. Trust me, you will refer to it often!

Shrink the Big Shadow

Let's just begin with the fact that a building at a major university is named after Dad. Consider that from a child's perspective, even (or perhaps especially) an adult child's. A permanent, imposing, over-whelmingly massive, architecturally striking, prominently located building is *named* after him! What must it take in terms of life ac-complishment for that to happen? (Not to mention donations to the school.) Trustees of these universities don't name buildings lightly.

Well, the father was remarkable in so many ways. Not only did he build a spectacularly successful company and sell it for many hundreds of millions of dollars, he wrote a bestselling novel and developed a successful patented product. Imagine the massive shadow he casts for his family! Imagine how impressive he seems up close and how most of the dreams and accomplishments of his children and grandchildren must pale in comparison, at least by their own estimation. Sure, Dad is charming and gregarious, opinionated, and often commanding. His energy and passion are palpable when he walks into a room. He never lacks for self-confidence, yet his kids are often riddled with doubts and questions about themselves.

Perhaps you grew up in a family in which one or more people were really and truly remarkable. There are stories and legends of their suc-cesses and feats. If you have someone like that in your lineage, you are fortunate, even more so if that person was also loving and available to you, present and forgiving, generous and compassionate, interested in your dreams. These big personalities, however, can cast even bigger shadows. The shadows are clear and formidable to the family mem-bers and virtually invisible to the people casting them. They often see themselves very differently than do their family members. They, of course, know well their own struggles, inadequacies, and failures, but they rarely talk of them. This means that they don't self-assess well the power of the shadows that they cast.

"*O.K., kid. Busy man here. Quality time. Here we go.*"

Jack Ziegler

One way that I often see the issue of the Big Shadow play out is in family enterprise legacies. Wealthy parents often look to their children as the flag bearers of their own dreams. They focus on how their kids can help them further their business or enterprise, hopes, legacy, or philanthropy. This is a powerful denial—masquerading as great opportunity and legacy—of who the child is as a person, and it is part and parcel of a Big Shadow subsuming their light.

Parents rarely, if ever, do this consciously. They see the family business or foundation as a terrific chance for the family to collaborate on a common dream, giving the children tremendous opportunities and ensuring family direction and control over the enterprises or charities the parents have formed. They see this as the ultimate sharing of important family values. *The unspoken truth, however, is that many children don't share the dreams of their parents.* They might not desire a bigger-than-life existence. They might have more modest ambitions for themselves and their families, more unassuming dreams.

WALL STREET VS MAIN STREET

Thomas, the eldest son of a powerful and dynamic partner in a Wall Street firm, was charming as a child and is utterly winning as a man. His father is a titan of finance in both the United States and abroad, consulted by presidents and Federal Reserve chairs. Thomas went to all the best schools, from an elite boarding school in New England to an Ivy League college and then to Wharton for his MBA. He had summer internships at his father's firm and entered the management training program upon graduation. His career, however, didn't live up to his father's dreams, nor to the firm's expectations. He had all the right ingredients, so to speak, so why wasn't this working? He was smart enough and fully capable, but he wasn't motivated enough or, perhaps worse for Wall Streeters, he wasn't "hungry" enough.

His father was initially patient but grew increasingly angry with his son's seemingly blasé attitude, and the other partners of the firm thought him a dilettante. Neither was true. Thomas was simply ill-suited for Wall Street. His dream was to be an architect and urban planner, but he felt so obligated to his father for the vast opportunities he'd been given, and he was so anxious to please his father, that he had agreed to the plan to join the firm. He'd rationalized the decision, as we often do when we make tremendous compromises. His friends were struggling to find jobs in their fields, many of them hadn't followed their true passions, and the salary was terrific by anyone's standards. Architecture could be his hobby, he reasoned. Perhaps he could design a house of his own one day.

Thomas eventually left the firm and followed his passion, a decision that was not without pain and emotional wounds. Over time, however, father and son were able to forge a strong and affectionate relationship. In fact, his parents are so proud of their son's work that they recently had Thomas design a new home for them.

Big Shadow, Small Person

The Big Shadow often looms large in non-business ways as well. My client Elizabeth is very recognizable and well regarded in the United States. Her face is on television often. She has two daughters in elementary school on whom she lavishes all kinds of fantastic opportunities and experiences. They travel extensively and attend cultural events all over the world. These are truly great opportunities for her children, but they have a very subtle negative impact. The Big Shadow that Elizabeth already casts is increased by the way she handles her time with her daughters: backstage at the *Nutcracker,* meeting the stars of every show and concert they see, photo ops with an incredible assortment of world dignitaries, chauffeured cars and private planes, exclusive screenings of blockbuster movies. Every conceivable privilege and exceptional moment is available to these children. Elizabeth uses her position to give her daughters bigger-than-life experiences over and over again. She says it feels like "payback" for her girls to have these treats, given the long hours she works and how often she has to be away from them.

While this sounds fantastic, it can be complicated. These experiences serve to increase the identity of the mother. *Elevation of the parent always runs the risk of diminishment of the child.* While the children feel special in so many ways during these events, at their core they surely realize that they are there only because of their mother. Furthermore, when you've repeatedly been in a box seat and backstage at the ballet, sitting in the audience becomes a lesser experience. The sense of self that such privileged kids can develop is a false self, hinged more to the accomplishments of their parents than to their own skills, talents, and interests. This "hinging up" to G1 is a common complication for the second generation, who compare their lives, accomplishments, choices, and successes and feel they come up short. The challenge for parents is to reduce the light that shines on them in favor of real and true and appropriate attention on the children.

Big Shadows also serve to separate children from their peers, and peers are an important connection for children to have as they develop. It's one thing to have the rare fabulous moment—meeting the president, photo op with your sports hero. But it's quite another to have your parents creating these moments for you, over and over again. How can your friends relate?

How do you know if you're casting a shadow that's too big? Ask yourself these questions:

- Do your children boast to their friends about who they met, who you are, who you know, or what terrific thing they did?

- Do they personalize possessions and opportunities as if they were their own? Do they say "my summer house" as opposed to "our" or "our family's"?

- Do you orchestrate repetitive fabulous experiences for them?

- Do your kids seem overly interested in you and your work? Kids are for the most part self-absorbed. Generally, they should be *far* more interested in themselves than in you.

- Think about how your life, your drive, your sense of self would have been impacted if your parents had frequently orchestrated "big moments" for you. Would it have motivated you more, or distracted you from discovering your own plans?

Money can buy many wonderful things, but happiness isn't one of them. When it comes to raising a child and providing the best possible childhood, part of your job as a parent is to teach that important lesson. Yes, you may be able to provide your child with many incredible, expensive things. You may be able to provide your child with many extraordinary experiences. But if you do this *all the time* you block out the reality for your child that money can't buy happiness. You need to equip your child to find happiness in the world regardless of whether there's money. That means teaching them to enjoy the bleachers as well as the box seats.

A Balancing Act

I understand that parents want to help their children reach their full potential. And I understand that parents dream big for their children. Where I often see difficulties arise in affluent families is when the dreams of the parents get in the way of the dreams of the child, and feelings of obligation and family duty chime in to further complicate the issue.

Deep complexity lies in the fact that children often feel so grateful and beholden to parents for the opportunities and advantages they've received that they end up essentially donating their lives to fulfilling the dreams of their parents. They accept positions in the family enterprises or subjugate their own dreams out of gratitude and deference to their family. Wealth advisor and attorney James Hughes describes the tension that exists between stewarding one's own dreams and spending time and energy stewarding the dreams of another. He believes that the second generation faces the challenge to integrate successfully two interrelated but very different realities; its own individual dreams and its inherited responsibility to be good stewards of the founder's dream."[5]

Here's the rub: family enterprises need continued family involvement if they are to stay rooted to the values and objectives upon which the founder conceived them. How, then, do affluent families encourage heirs to pursue their own values and dreams while at the same time providing the continuity and security of family direction to the family business? Talk about balancing acts! When inheritors devote their energy and passions to their parents' or grandparents' dreams, leaving only a small slice of their lives to their own dreams and passions, that equilibrium can become seriously distorted and lead to lives of deep disappointment and pain.

In the absence of a family member who genuinely shares the dreams of the founder and wants to work in the enterprise, external management and family-controlled boards with external directors often work well. However, I believe some family members will never spend time in the family business affairs because it is not their interest or not in their skill set. However, it is my experience that even family members that are disinclined can benefit enormously from giving some appropriate attention to the operations, and finances, of their family. I believe it is both appropriate and healthy for heirs to spend increasing amounts of time in family business affairs as they age. My rule of thumb is that those in their twenties and thirties, who are presumably beginning their own careers and starting their own families, should devote no more than 5 percent of their time to the family enterprise (in a working month, this equals one day's worth of time, twelve days a year, or two and a half work weeks a year). In their forties and fifties, when work and families are becoming a bit more established, their family enterprise commitment might grow to 10 percent of their time, which is 24 days a year or 2 days a month. Those in their sixties and seventies can bump it to 20 to 50 percent of their time or more, depending on their goals and interest. Again, this is assuming that the heir is fulfilling a responsibility and a legacy, not that they are independently passionate about the enterprise. If someone is truly passionate, then of course they can devote their lives to the family business.

If an heir has other passions and interests, asking them to spend even 10 percent of their time on a family enterprise could deeply affect their choice of careers, ability to advance, reputation in their field, and time available for their family. I often see second and third generations working hard to keep their wealthy status private from their coworkers, lest they be seen as less deserving or less motivated. One professor I know tried very hard to keep his coworkers from seeing his house, a lovely home in an affluent neighborhood that he couldn't possibly have afforded on his academic salary. He felt sure it would impact how they felt about his seriousness and commitment to his work. He may well have been right, but holding that secret also served to separate him from his work community.

I firmly believe that it's up to the parents and grandparents to seek to know the passions of their children and grandchildren; only then can they accurately assess whether the family enterprise might be where they should devote their time. Asking the children themselves to make this determination is fraught with complexity. Heirs are mired in obligation, ego, and gratitude that inhibit their ability to be completely honest, either to themselves or with their elders. The "gift" that these inheritors have been given complicates their ability to see the situation clearly. The older set must support and even encourage a process of discovery and exploration around true passions and interests.

Parenting is the best, hardest, and most important piece to creating a family who flourishes. My advice is to seize that work with gusto and passion. Keep your feet on the ground and your attention on your children and who they are. Focus on all the ways that you can lift your kids up to realize their dreams, not on how they can help you extend your own. Make time in your busy life for them to be important. Allow them to impress you, or even better, to overshadow you.

When I cut to the chase, through all of my
strategies and counsel, I find one overarching
truth: the secret to a thriving, connected family
is focused, intentional parenting.

THREE

PITCH A BIG TENT

"Happiness is having a large, loving, caring, close-knit family in another city."
—GEORGE BURNS

Most families, from all walks of life, possess core values that motivate their behaviors, define their worldview, and animate their relationships. These values derive from many sources, including religion, philosophy, and the study of economic/political history. They've been learned from parents, teachers, and mentors; honed by life experiences and crystalized in the cauldron of family dynamics.

Strong, healthy families generally have well-defined, clearly articulated, life-affirming values. In such families, values are discussed openly, lived enthusiastically, constitute the organizing principle of family life, and define the nature and quality of many family relationships.

I have come to believe that openness, clarity, and intentionality about family values for wealthy multigenerational families is a sine qua non for flourishing. Accordingly, this chapter focuses on how such families identify their values, learn to express them, live them, and develop productive ways to make them accessible and appealing to their children and grandchildren.

Families who develop interfamilial communication skills, build trust, and are able to experience meaningful connection are well equipped to explore the topic of shared family values. I have discovered that families can benefit enormously by focusing on three important core principles related to their values:

- Know the difference between values and preferences
- Live your values
- Determine which values matter most

Values vs Preferences

Wealthy individuals have the luxury of being able to live in a way that is completely reflective of their values. They don't have the obligatory distractions that financial insecurity can create. They can choose how to spend each day, month, even year, and as such can express their values through the manner in which they live their lives. Indeed, their values are on bold display in the choices they make around how to allocate their time and resources.

In recent years, "family values" has become a bit of a catchphrase. You hear it everywhere—even on TV commercials—as relates to politics, philanthropy, global conflict, religion. Everyone, it seems, wants to question the "family values" that some individual or organization supposedly holds. We can't seem to escape this obsession with, and evaluation of, the values of others. It provides a lens through which we assess far too many issues, and individuals.

I'm often called by families interested in learning about ways to successfully pass their values down to the next generations. The parents feel they were raised with strong anchoring and orienting values, and wish to ensure that their children, being brought up in much greater affluence, get a solid grounding in values.

These parents both believe that their values have contributed to the quality of their lives and to their success, and they are seeking an insurance policy against wealth itself becoming a core value that distracts and even harms their children. They're looking for ways to guard their family from the risks associated with deep pockets. Successful entrepreneurs are generally skilled at identifying risk and finding ways to ameliorate it—that's one reason they've been successful!—so it follows that they look for ways to address and reduce the risks associated with passing wealth to their children. This particular form of risk management can be expressed in family values statements, trust documents, mission statements, prenuptial agreements, training and jobs for their kids, and in many other ways.

But it's easier to pass down money than it is to pass down values, unless you have a plan and attend to it with the same thought as you do the wealth management. In fact, the manner in which one generation passes down its values often reflects the same philosophy and attitudes they exhibit toward the transfer of wealth.

For example, someone who passes down the value of compassion and service will likely also pass down assets to charity; someone who passes down the value of hard work and productivity to their children likely will not create an estate plan that allows the heirs to remain jobless. Those who believe in generosity will use their estate plan to be generous to their family and world, while those who are controlling and fearful are likely to use their wealth to "operationalize" those values.

GOOD IDEA GONE BAD

Jim was deeply worried about his son. They'd been close when young Jim Jr. was a child and even into his early teens, but since he'd turned seventeen things had changed. "JJ" was different—cool, more remote, interested in "weird" things, including a number of liberal causes. Crazy stuff, Jim Sr. thought, and potentially quite troublesome.

Jim consulted with a number of people who'd known JJ for years—his school counselor, the family lawyer, his older siblings, his wife, even the parish priest. Everyone seemed to think JJ was fine, perhaps just trying to find himself. But Jim's worries persisted.

Suddenly Jim had an idea. He'd established a foundation a few years prior to give to a number of causes about which he was passionate. He decided to engage JJ by offering to fund something he cared about. He was sure this was a great way to connect with JJ, spend some time together, teach him about philanthropy, and help him see the benefit of his (Jim Sr.'s) core values.

He called a family meeting, and proudly announced his goal of getting the kids more involved in the foundation and his plan to give each of them $15,000 to give toward a worthy cause that they would research and present to the family board. He gave them all three months to do this.

Jim Sr. offered JJ help on the project, as he was the youngest and least experienced with charity, but JJ consistently declined his father's involvement. He was actually silent on the subject, to the point that his parents were sure he'd forgotten about it. The next meeting opened, as usual, with the trust officer from the bank reviewing the recent investment performance and proposed tax changes. The agenda then turned to the foundation grants. Jim's two older children presented their research and proposals: a grant to a new local Catholic elementary school and a grant for an entrepreneurial studies program at the college the eldest had attended.

Then JJ distributed his research. He had clearly spent weeks on his proposal. It was very well researched, documented, and articulated. They were floored. He'd appeared uninterested, but in fact was completely engaged and passionate about philanthropy!

The proposed recipient of his gift, however, was shocking to Jim. JJ proposed contributing to a new local AIDS clinic. Jim was furious. Everyone knew he held deep and fervent conservative values! This was a slap in the face. He left the meeting after granting his older daughters the money for their grants and rejecting JJ's. Jim slammed the door on his way out, mumbling about his son's defiant values.

This is a clear example of what can go wrong when wealth holders confuse the process of passing down family values with passing down individual preferences and attitudes. Jim Sr. wanted to create philanthropic opportunity for his children as a way of teaching them the family value of philanthropy. Philanthropy can be an inspired, appropriate way to pass down the value of caring for others. I've seen it work very well in many families, but Jim Sr. missed the mark when he responded negatively to JJ's choice of philanthropy. He mistook JJ's choice as a rejection of their family values when it was, in fact, just the opposite: JJ was embracing the family value of philanthropy. What he didn't embrace was his father's preference for more traditional or conservative charities. Jim Sr. confused values for preferences, a mistake made by many wealth owners. You can try to teach your children values, but you can't impose your preferences on them. They must learn and embrace their preferences on their own.

In any discussion about values, clarifying the distinction between values and preferences is critical. A "value" is a deeply held core principle or belief, whereas a "preference," or attitude, is the way in which a value is actually expressed.

Some common values and our preferences for expressing them:

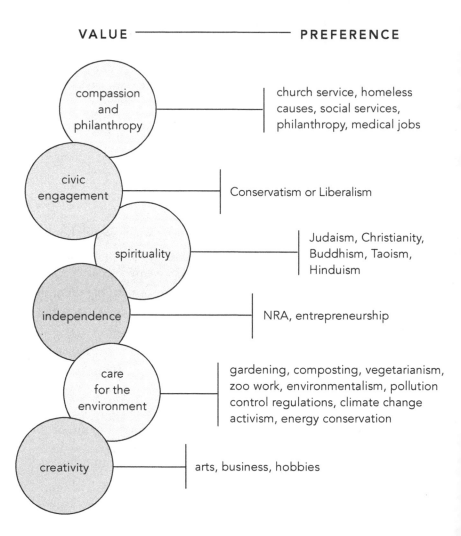

VALUE ——————————— PREFERENCE

compassion and philanthropy — church service, homeless causes, social services, philanthropy, medical jobs

civic engagement — Conservatism or Liberalism

spirituality — Judaism, Christianity, Buddhism, Taoism, Hinduism

independence — NRA, entrepreneurship

care for the environment — gardening, composting, vegetarianism, zoo work, environmentalism, pollution control regulations, climate change activism, energy conservation

creativity — arts, business, hobbies

Live Your Values

Once they have worked to clarify their values, I ask my clients to take a hard look at themselves. Are their values congruent with their own behavior? Have they aligned the important values they hold with the way they go about their business each day? Are their activities consistent with their words?

Scrutinizing personal and family values can prove double-edged. At best, values can be a good way to think about what matters to you, a compass of clarity that can help you choose among a variety of life paths and individual daily decisions on how to spend your time and money. It can be good grounding for interfamilial relationships and for how we interact with others socially, politically, and at work. At the very least, it serves as a lens to understand another person.

At worst, depending on what the values are, how they are defined, and how they are communicated, a parent's clarity about his or her values can strip others, most often children, of their identity and individuality. Strong feelings about values can even become a weapon of sorts, threatening superiority and judgment. Do the very wealthy somehow feel that their values are preferable to others? Perhaps. But don't we all think our values and priorities are best? That's human nature. What becomes complicated and often troublesome is when parents have the motivation and means to insist that their values are embraced and, what's more, when they expect their children to pass their values down to future generations. The leaders of wealthy families (and particularly the wealth creator) hold power positions in their families, so discussions about values can be complicated and highly charged. In these families, conversations about values can really be about power, worthiness, and control.

Arnie Levin

Families who flourish actually embrace and embed their values into their family's dynamics. Values are practically in their DNA. First, they identify the values they hold dearest, then they find language and actions that express them clearly, and eventually they focus on the few that they believe are core to their family's well-being.

In addition to recognizing your values, it is critically important to engage in actions that promote them in your life on a regular basis. Think of this as the difference between theoretical values and operational values—those we aspire to (theoretical) versus those we actually live (operational). Dr. R. Kelly Crace of Duke University has spent nearly thirty years studying values, life satisfaction, and resilience. His research points to the critical importance of committing to one's core values and the role doing so plays in resilience and flourishing.

Integrity, the alignment of our behavior to our values, is one of the cornerstones of adult self-esteem. The more we are intentional about our values, the better we are able to adjust our behavior accordingly and become more aware of the fears and challenges that intrude upon that alignment. This process of intentionality and adjustment fosters a sense of fulfillment and resilience that can withstand enormous stress without feeling strained.[6]

The clearer parents are about the values they care most about passing on, the more actions they should be able to associate with them. A simple example of this revolves around spirituality—if that is a high value in your family, then regular spiritual or religious practice is crucial. If hard work and productivity are important values, then your family likely requires all teens to have chores and/or summer jobs and will not provide so much access to money that the heirs don't have to work for a living.

There is a risk here. I've worked with countless families in which passing down the values of the elder generation takes on outsized importance. Elders frequently use it as a benchmark to judge the success of their children. They seek not to understand and embrace the values of their children, but rather to shoehorn their own values into their children. They miss the crucial truth: a successful life is one in which you live consistent with your values, not necessarily with the values of your father or mother or grandparent.

Wealth often allows some elders to feel entitled to attempt this "values infusion" in more controlling and sometimes domineering ways than I see in middle-class families. The (oft-unstated) dialogue goes something like this: "I've given you everything you could have ever dreamed of—the finest education, travel, material possessions, money of your own. All I ask in return is that you lead a responsible life, a life that reflects the opportunities that you've been given." The rhetoric is both nuanced and damaging. The guilt that this implied contract creates ("I gave you everything, so you owe me") denies the individual and creates a kind of servitude. At its worst, it demands the donating of one's own self to the greater good of the family. Moreover, it's hard for the outside world to empathize or even understand, seeing as how everything looks so good. But the beautiful packaging, so to speak, disguises a very hurtful "gift."

Bucking Our Cultural Tide

We live in an outcome-focused culture. Our young people are constantly, incessantly, and sometimes obsessively trained to produce outcomes. The values that parents, society and institutions focus on are the outcome values—productivity, responsibility, academic and financial success, and achievement. We even manage to turn compassion into an outcome value when we use a student's history of volunteering to assess their college application. This creates unbelievable stress within and among children. They see their self-worth as directly tied to what they do, what they can control. The parent's job, says Dr. Crace, is to be the voice that balances all of the outcome stress and to help children focus on the process of life and living instead of the outcomes. Parents should help their children cultivate more of the "why" of life, not merely the "what," he explains. Look foremost at the journey, not the destination. Consider the satisfaction and enjoyment an experience provides, not the result alone.

Many successful people thrive on outcomes. They love the "win" that accomplishing great things brings. But what Dr. Crace further suggests is that parents should endeavor to help their children understand and develop their own values, their own compass, their own life path, and not encourage them to follow a path that the parents have imagined for them.

Herein lies a perfect storm: an implosion of angst brought on by the parents' inherent outcome focus combined with overarching concern that their kids haven't inherited their values (and will therefore be damaged by their wealth, fail to live up to their potential, or leave the family enterprise in the hands of non-family members). Amped-up parents then push their values even harder. I'm sure you can guess where this leads.

Parents often call me after the storm, wondering where they went wrong. Their young adult son is a progressive, almost-Buddhist artist. This, in a family of conservative, entrepreneurial Catholic Republicans! Or the devoutly Jewish business family has just been introduced to their daughter's serious (currently unemployed) boyfriend, who was raised in a vegan, atheist, and environmental-activist family. Where did they go wrong? How could they have failed so miserably to pass on the most important values they have?

Again, these parents are confusing values with preferences. They simply can't see that their children did indeed inherit their values—and at the highest level—and are expressing compassion, social engagement, spirituality, hard work, honesty, and integrity. It's just that they're expressing them in ways that are relevant for them.

Instead of seeing their children as having differing preferences, attitudes, or expressions of their values, they see their children as having opposing values. Considerable amounts of family tension might be avoided if only parents could see this distinction more clearly.

Families who flourish link actions in their home to such values, and leave plenty of room for individual expression of preferences. They are intentional and consistent in expressing their own values and preferences and shine the light on what they do and why they do it. They explain why they make the choices that they make and link it back to their values. None of this is subtle. But they also allow for a broad definition of "acceptable" when it comes to talking about values. And they embrace the diversity of ideas and choices in their family well.

Determine Which Values Matter Most

The values that matter most to many of the families I have worked with over the years could not be more basic. They ask, "How do I raise grounded, responsible, motivated/productive, and compassionate children?" They tell me that these are their values and they were also the values of their parents and grandparents. However, now that there is significant wealth, they worry that the money and the lifestyle are spoiling their children.

Grounded

What does "grounded" really look like? Living a life surrounded by fine things, enriching opportunities, and the trappings of privilege is great. Fine cuisine, lovely homes, safety and security, beauty—all contribute to a rich and wonderful life. How, then, can we raise kids who are hard-working, empathetic, and able to relate to the broader, more diverse world around them? How can we be sure we don't raise spoiled, entitled, and closed-minded kids?

The more parents can expose their kids to diverse yet mainstream human experiences and conditions the better. Friends from various economic and social strata help a lot, but unless the parents themselves have friends from a wide range of backgrounds and circumstances, it isn't enough. Over the years I've had clients call me with a similar dilemma: their child attends a local parochial/public school and is being teased about the family wealth. The parents or grandparents are, say, highly visible citizens, and there are numerous outward signs of the family wealth in the community. The parents are looking for ways their child can respond when targeted for derision. Underlying their concern is a bigger question: should their child perhaps attend a different school, one in which he or she might be more like the other kids? My short answer, always, is do whatever you can to mainstream your child. Don't create a gated community around them lest they become narrow and scared, or reject your lifestyle altogether and break free of its constraints. Create the opportunities in your own life to interact meaningfully and authentically with a wide range of people from varying circumstances.

In many cases, the enchanted world around these children bolsters the notion that they are unique, different, or even very special. A young woman I know who attended one of D.C.'s elite private schools once told me she worried about "letting down her school community" when her career dreams were more modest than the global stage for which she'd been prepared. In *Privilege: The Making of an Adolescent Elite at St. Paul's School,* Shamus Rahman Khan describes the way in which students are routinely schooled to see themselves as "the elite." Students are taught to think of their research papers as "contributions to the world's knowledge." A student with a strong track record in a particular sport is widely considered by his classmates to be a contender for a national championship. "This kind of assumption—that the best student in each particular subject at St. Paul's was probably the best person in the world—was widespread," asserts Khan. This attitude, while perhaps admirable on some level, can create a super-sized ego, a tremendous outcome orientation, and the possibility of launching students who are destined to feel inadequate when their reality falls short of the future they were groomed to inhabit.

How can successful parents keep their kids from becoming elitist? Dr. Ned Hallowell, an advisor to numerous independent schools, had the following to say when I asked him about groundedness versus elitism.

> *Keep your kids in the main of life, don't create cocoon lives for them in which they are always in the "best" of everything . . . hotels, restaurants, vacations, performances, neighborhoods. Let them be in the flow of life, connecting with many who are like them and many who are not. Think about how you explain "not rich" to them. Have fun with them, a lot of fun. Embrace parenting with the zeal that you embrace business.*

If you want to raise children who are grounded, you must resist some of the accoutrements and ease that can come with success. This can be hard, as it requires the adults to forgo these wonderful benefits as well. I often tell the story about a family in which no member of the third generation—nineteen children ranging in age from two months to twenty-four years—had ever flown on a commercial airline. The entirety of their air travel had been on family planes. They'd never had the oh-so-humbling experience of being stranded at O'Hare on a stormy night, or rebooked to a city only mildly convenient for them. They'd never rented a car to drive home instead or scrounged for (and been tearfully grateful for) a lousy hotel room when the airport was closed down due to weather. Such challenging experiences develop character, resilience, and resourcefulness.

When adults—whether parents or pilots—jump to meet their every need, children get a clear message of entitlement. More significant, however, is the stifling of their resilience and competence, which in turn hinders their full maturation. When you're left with little other than your own ingenuity and determination, you find out just how much you can really accomplish. What a shame to take that away from a child by solving their every problem and inconvenience. Finding solutions and learning how to cope is a fundamental step toward maturity and can so easily be missed when teams of people stand ready to serve and accommodate.

When family lawyers, accountants, and office execs ask me how they can best serve the next generation of the family, I often respond, "Leave them be for as long as possible." Don't help them with college applications, renting apartments, arranging for utilities service, buying a car, etc. Adults already have to help them open bank and investment accounts, prepare their taxes, and deal with legal documents. Let them struggle with a few things—it's good for them! As they say, good judgment comes from experience, and experience comes from bad judgment. *If we don't give inheritors a chance to make a few mistakes, they won't have the experience or confidence necessary when it comes time for them to take control of their financial lives in more substantial ways.*

It's important to note a developmental truth here—when we allow others to leap in and "over-function" for our kids, solving many of the problems they could solve for themselves given time and encouragement, the message they receive is that they're incompetent or, perhaps worse, can't be trusted. We think we're demonstrating love for them, but they interpret it as fixing problems for them because they themselves cannot.

Responsible

What's the difference between being grounded and being responsible? In my view, grounded is a state of mind. It's how you see yourself in the world and how you compare yourself to others. Responsible, on the other hand, is a state of being that's expressed in your actions, not by your mind-set.

If you want to raise responsible children, then they need to be held accountable for their actions and given many chances to both fail and succeed. They need ample opportunities to learn new concepts, mess things up, and improve and perform consistently. This could be through school, sports, jobs, or chores. So while this may seem straightforward, it gets more complicated in the face of wealth and privilege.

For instance, hobbies are often serial in nature and short-lived in affluent families. A young girl shows some interest in playing the violin and so a tutor is hired, a violin is purchased, and the lessons begin. Wow, it's way harder than she thought it would be! The practicing wanes. The girl waffles in her enthusiasm. She suggests that the violin isn't the right instrument for her. The parents protest. She discovers a newly found love of the piano. The parents hesitate, but then imagine how wonderful it would have been to have learned piano themselves. Still, they hesitate. But the girl persists. And so a piano teacher is found. An electronic keyboard is purchased. The pattern is established. The same can occur with summer jobs (when they actually happen) and household chores. There are always extenuating circumstances to prevent the child from following through and completing the job or chore.

Because there are so often extra hands that help the wealthy and successful accomplish daily responsibilities, young people can miss the chance to learn those skills. It is true that the ability to care for one's self and others creates a sense of competence and responsibility, from the mundane tasks of laundry and cooking to the more complex tasks of identifying, acquiring, and succeeding in a job. Additionally, the element of having others depend on you is a crucial step in the development of well-functioning adult.

Just because you can afford to serve up a new instrument every few months doesn't mean you should. Just because you have household help who can do the chores doesn't mean they should. Just because your child doesn't need the money that they earn from a job doesn't mean they shouldn't have one. And last, just because you can afford to give them the world doesn't mean that it's good for them that you do.

"Someday, you may thank me for breaking what was becoming, in this family, a viscous cycle of inheritance!"

Productive / Motivated

If you want to raise productive children, then you can't just give them everything. Doing so robs them of the self-satisfaction and competence that comes from being productive. They have to long for and strive for things they can attain only through their own hard work and commitment. I find that parents (many of the Depression era) who have been successful through much hard work often resist allowing their children to struggle themselves. They see helping them generously as giving them a leg up. The problem is they never feel the thrill and satisfaction that comes from one's own achievements. There are, however, large and small ways in which a parent can help their children become productive. A big one is the summer job.

In wealthy families, summer jobs are often a sore spot. The family is traveling and the family reunion is in mid-August and, besides, it's hard to find a job, and the really good jobs are all taken, and the jobs should really be left for those who truly need the money, etc., etc. The end result is a whole slew of college graduates, even post-grads, who've never had a real job. They have fabulous resumes full of enriching "experiences," but no down-and-dirty work.

So they've missed the opportunity to feel a sense of satisfaction and accomplishment—big deal! They've been to Africa and Asia and volunteered in South America while on vacation with their parents. But the truth is, it *is* a big deal. I've been told by Ivy League college admissions staff that "African volunteering" on a college application, *unaccompanied by any real summer jobs,* is a red flag that screams "pampered." Real-world jobs, as opposed to pseudo jobs (working in the family business or for a family friend), are crucially important, with responsibility—and competency-building components. Your children will learn more valuable life skills waiting tables for three months than on a safari.

Working for a family business can be beneficial if a few important elements are in place:

- The young person must be objectively qualified for the position. This usually means they begin in an entry-level position.

- They must—and I can't emphasize this enough—they *must* report to a non-family member who has the authority to fire them if they don't perform. And that person must have the moral character and job security to actually manage them well.

- They have to adhere to the same hours, compensation, and requirements as all other comparable employees—no special treatment.

- They must be willing to work as hard as, or harder than, everyone else.

Young people who have acquired a job and been compensated for that work are infinitely more competent and responsible than those who have not. These young people have a sense of being able to care for themselves. They're more resilient and have a stronger idea of their own self-worth. They have a chance to learn what they like and dislike about certain kinds of work. They also have the satisfaction and freedom that comes with financial remuneration. They're not dependent upon the generosity or largesse of their parents for everything they do. They can make financial choices that are their own.

Compassionate

Parents often believe that the best way to instill empathy in their children is to give them money for charity to help them learn the fundamentals of giving. This may be especially true for wealthy families. But true empathy requires getting outside of one's self and typically stems from getting ample love and attention from one's parents. Children who have highly busy, self-absorbed parents are rarely able to tend well to the needs of anyone else because they haven't been given enough emotional nurturing and attention themselves. Highly successful adults can also be self-focused, highly ego-driven, and only limitedly available to their children. The first step toward developing compassionate children is to be emotionally and physically available to them.

Once your children have received the love and attention that serve as a foundational basis of compassion, they need to be shown, by you(!), empathy and generosity toward others. The compassion you teach your children should be overt and obvious. Bring your charity and philanthropy out of the office. Roll up your shirtsleeves and make sure your child bears witness. Show them how important and constant your own compassion is, and how gratifying it is to connect to others in this way. All the better if it's about connection, not noblesse oblige, and about how we love one another, not about our duty to give based on how much we have. The former promises possibility and energy, while the latter is subject to the downward spiral of obligation and burden.

Exciting your children about helping others and about being a citizen of the world is important work. "The problems of our world are vast and deep and complex," writes Craig Kilburger, founder of Free the Children. "We need those who have resources of any kind—intellect, creativity, wealth, position, power, courage, and faith—to lean in and help others." [7]

If motivated and encouraged, the children of the affluent can affect so much in the world. The impact they have grows exponentially if their parents collaborate. There are literally thousands of ways to do this, from church-based programs and community-based nonprofits to national and international programs. Put energy and resources toward giving back and the benefits your children and the greater world will reap will be substantial and profound.

Another facet of compassion is one that is rarely, if ever, discussed—openheartedness. Raising children to have the capacity for love, vulnerability, honesty, and joy is a deeply worthy endeavor. Imagine the world we would live in if we raised a generation with this ideal rather than one based predominantly on success and privilege.

What makes a real difference in the sustainability of the family? What makes family members far more likely to remain connected over time? How can you increase the likelihood that your children and grandchildren will both thrive and seek a deep relationship with you and toward one another? How can you avoid values-based fights with your child? The answer to all of these questions: embrace diversity!

Be curious about those who are not naturally like you, both in and out of the family. Learn to see differing opinions as ballast in the "family ship," a spread of skills, knowledge, traits, and characters that create a broad and resilient family. Differences can oft times be used as a way to draw lines in the sand. Citing differences forces us to identify those who are "like us" (and by default those who are not). It forces us to choose "our people." We use our values and opinions to define ourselves and what is important to us. Frequently, however, the narrow definition and judgments that accompany this kind of thinking don't serve the individuals or the family. Not only do we teach our children bias and judgment, but we limit the kinds of wonderful differences that we can have in our lives. And the tent shrinks.

The implications of a smaller tent are extremely detrimental to individual family members and to the sustainability and resilience of the family as a whole. When others feel excluded from your tent, they feel that the family sees them as different in an unacceptable way. They feel judged and "less than" other family members. To see where such feelings might exist in your family, discuss the many types of diversity—gender, political, ethnic, religious, lifestyle, sexual orientation, economic, intellectual, ideological, vocational, and priorities—that you encounter in life. Think and talk with your family about the ways in which a "Big Tent" allows for freedom of individuality.

Ask your children, parents, or siblings to share the ways in which they feel accepted for their differences and where they feel judged. If your family hasn't been accepting of differences, then this could take years to accomplish. Furthermore, the elders have to be sincerely open to diversity, not just window-dressing a critical attitude.

Simply stated, small tents with hard rules of inclusion encourage outcast family members to look for new tents. If they can't be themselves in their own family, and be valued for their uniqueness, they'll look for people with whom they can create a "new family." That's a tragedy I frequently see, and it's so easy to avoid. Open your arms wide to the daughter-in-law who comes from a very different economic background or religion. Embrace the child who has much more liberal views and choices. Parents who feel they have failed to instill their values, and that the family strength and identity are jeopardized by differences, are missing out. Your family is far more apt to remain connected over time if there is a place at the table for all.

Wealthy individuals have the luxury of being able to live in a way that is completely reflective of their values.

FOUR

BECOME
EMOTIONALLY FLUENT

*"Let's not forget that the little emotions
are the great captains of our lives and
we obey them without realizing it."*

—VINCENT VAN GOGH

We've talked about creating systems that support communication, making time for family, being intentional in parenting, exploring our cherished values, and embracing diversity. But we haven't done the hardest work. While all of this requires self-knowledge, it doesn't focus directly on the importance of deeper personal and emotional exploration. We haven't looked within.

During my twenty years advising families worth tens of millions, hundreds of millions, and even billions of dollars, I have listened to and counseled individuals who are wealth creators, inheritors, investors, artists, full-time mothers, managers, teachers, academics, active non-profit volunteers, business managers, executives, professionals, and occasionally those unemployed seeking work.

Wealthy people are not immune to the complex and often difficult vagaries of life, nor are they insulated from the consequences of human error, bad luck, or poor decisions. It is of course true that they have more financial resources to devote to solving their problems, but they don't always possess the skills, emotional intelligence, or psychological resources necessary to fix what is broken in their personal lives.

Not everyone is sympathetic to the needs, hopes, trials, and tribulations of families of wealth. Indeed, many I encounter are surprised that the wealthy actually have family matters they want and need to address thoughtfully and with professionals, while others have been downright dismissive of the work I do.

An underlying theme seems to be that wealth should make you blissfully happy all of the time, solve all of your problems by its very existence, and/or preclude the need for the hard work to know oneself, build meaningful relationships, strengthen family bonds, and contribute to a healthy society.

I, of course, disagree. I firmly believe that the search for connection, trust, self-awareness, familial harmony, and joy defines our humanity, and is not a journey limited by the measure of our wealth, status, or privilege. This quest to belong, to be respected, to be productive, and to have dignity is both quintessential and universal.

But sometimes the emotional challenges facing families of wealth get short shrift. *How can they possibly be unhappy with all that money? If I had that much money, no one in my family would ever be unhappy again.* Unfortunately, that stereotype is held by many, even by some in wealthy families themselves. People who see things in this way tend to brush off the emotional challenges of wealth as trivial or overblown.

This chapter asks you to put aside that notion and to look at some of the emotional challenges related to wealth and how to meet them. It's neither useful nor rational to pretend these challenges don't exist. No one knows better than families with money that money can't buy happiness. Happiness requires another level of effort—an emotional effort.

I've worked with families who possess a wide range of emotional skills and I've learned that emotional intelligence is a sine qua non for maintaining a happy family in the midst of affluence. To create a family who thrives both financially and emotionally, family members must strive to be emotionally fluent. In this chapter, we'll examine what that means and how to achieve it. Specifically we will explore:

- Vulnerability
- Family Systems Theory
- Trust
- Hurdles

A New Language

I define "emotional fluency" as the ability and willingness to feel and express a full range of authentic emotions without blame or judgment and to be able to hear and learn the true feelings of others.

Many of us have been exposed to the concept of an Emotional Quotient (EQ)—a measure of emotional intelligence. We've been told that it's just as important as IQ when it comes to being a high-functioning individual. Emotional intelligence can be seen in a number of ways. For example, can you express anger and then let it go? Can you receive help as well as give it? Can you say no without feeling guilty? Can you be vulnerable? Can you listen to others and hear their pain and fear? These are all elements of emotional intelligence.

Emotional fluency takes this type of emotional expression a step further. Emotional fluency often revolves around the management—and liberation—of one's own emotions and openness to others. Do you allow yourself to frequently experience pleasure? Do you sometimes feel moved by the courage or the spirit of others?

Can you contain (rather than repress) your impulses and delay your gratification, without resorting to guilt, shame, or suppression of your emotions? Do you often laugh out loud? Can you see the hidden motivations that you have? How about those that others have? Do you understand your emotional triggers? These are the actions of an emotionally fluent individual.

For families of means, money is frequently a highly emotional issue, one linked to emotional relationships among parents, children, siblings, cousins, and spouses. With money so woven into the emotional tapestry of the wealthy, it's no surprise that the ability to understand and manage these emotions is vital. Without emotional fluency, much of the smart and sophisticated structural work of succession plans, family meetings, wills, and trusts falls apart. And yet, deeply examining our feelings is often a task we fear, diminish, and too frequently avoid.

The Role of Vulnerability

So many issues we face in life boil down to wanting, and needing, to be loved. Sibling rivalry stems from wondering which child Mom and Dad love most, for instance. The ability to experience and embrace joy is also about love. Am I loved enough to be open to happiness? When we get trapped in a self-protective pattern of avoiding vulnerability, we can be psychologically stuck by a lack of self-worth. We hide the parts of ourselves we believe make us unlovable. We convince ourselves that we'll be rejected if others see our doubts, inadequacies, and weaknesses. Research, however, shows that the very act of living with and owning our vulnerability makes us more open and accepting of ourselves, and as such more loving and accepting of others. We are all drawn to those who are authentic and comfortable with themselves, who allow us to see inside the veneer to the truer self.

Dr. Brené Brown, a University of Houston researcher, contends that those who are able to be open and love fully are essentially those who believe they are worthy of being loved fully. She contends that it's their vulnerabilities, not their strengths, that make them lovable. *How about that!?* Most of us move through our lives trying to hide, deny, and reject our perceived weaknesses, when it's those very vulnerabilities that could be the key to love and acceptance.

Willing oneself into accepting that our most shameful weaknesses could ever be a part of what makes us lovable is a particularly vexing problem for the wealthy and successful, who often feel a need to "protect" themselves and their families (and their image) from others. Most of us are inclined to protect ourselves from the embarrassment and shame of showing our perceived weaknesses, but the successful often work even harder to hide their vulnerabilities. If only they could realize what Dr. Brown's research illuminates.

> *Our imperfections are what connect us to each other and to our humanity. Our vulnerabilities are not weaknesses; they are powerful reminders to keep our hearts and minds open to the reality that we are all in this together.*[8]

I can't help but applaud Brown's use of that all-important word, "connect," which I posit in Chapter 1 as the emotional foundation of families who flourish.

Family Systems Theory

There are, thankfully, systematic ways to seek out and achieve emotional fluency. Dr. Murray Bowen is considered the father of the Family Systems Theory, much like Freud is thought of as the father of individual therapy. In the 1950's Bowen began his work on the study of families at Georgetown University (it was later moved outside the university) where I studied for years. What I learned there has changed the way I work and live and love; moreover, it truly altered my understanding of families.

Bowen sees the family as an emotionally complex system. And, he notes, as in any system, if one part changes, the entire system shifts to adapt to that change. Additionally, an understanding of any family system requires the deep understanding of the emotional, biological, and environmental influences that individuals and families have had to accommodate over generations. The following eight concepts form the cornerstone of Bowen's theory and, he contends, affect the balance between togetherness and individuality:

> **1. Differentiation of self.** Families and other social groups affect how people think, act, and feel, but individuals vary in their sensitivity to "group think." The less developed a person's "self," the more impact others have on his or her functioning and the more he or she tries to control the functioning of others. Groups vary in the amount of pressure they try to exert on any one person to conform.

> **2. Nuclear family.** Bowen believes that the nuclear family embodies the most intense set of emotional relationships in one's life. He describes four relationships where problems usually develop in a family: (a) marital conflict, (b) dysfunction in one spouse, (c) impairment of one or more children, and/or (d) emotional distance between individuals.

> **3. Family projection process.** This concept describes the way parents transfer their emotional problems onto a child. Some parents have difficulty emotionally separating from their child. They imagine how the child is, rather than having an objective opinion. The parental processes that most negatively affect a child's life are a heightened need for attention and approval, difficulty dealing with expectations, a tendency to blame (oneself or others), feeling responsible for other's happiness, and acting impulsively to relieve the anxiety of the moment rather than tolerating anxiety and acting thoughtfully.

> **4. Multigenerational transmission process.** Bowen's concept here is how small differences in the levels of differentiation between parents and their children can lead, when observed over many

generations, to important differences in differentiation among the members of a multigenerational family. Simply stated, if individuals can improve the way in which they maintain a sense of themselves within their family, then that small shift can lead to healthier families over generations. For most of us, being authentically ourselves is most challenging when we are with our parents and siblings. We feel the most pressure to conform, the most "triggered" by their reactions, and the least independent. What Bowen believes is that to whatever degree we can hold our own in that family dynamic, the better the family can thrive over time.

5. Sibling position. Psychologist Walter Toman's work on sibling position informs Bowen's theory in important ways. They both believe that people who grow up in the same sibling position have important common characteristics. For example, oldest children tend to more naturally be leaders, whereas youngest children often prefer to be followers. Toman's research shows that spouses' sibling positions, when mismatched, often increase the likelihood of difficulty in their marriage.[9] As an example, an eldest son works well in a marriage with a younger daughter if he had a younger sister. And a youngest daughter who has an older brother knows well how to relate to someone in that "position." In essence, they've already learned how to be in a relationship with this dynamic. What works less well is when two youngest children marry, since neither of them innately knows how to relate to the other.

6. Triangles. Triangles create a three-person relationship in which inherent relational tension is managed, for better or worse, by the dynamic among the three. For example, a mother, father, and child form a triangle in which tension is often handled when one individual smooths the relationship between the other two members. A less positive example is when one sibling forms a triangle with parents to keep another sibling on the "outside."

7. Emotional cutoff. People sometimes manage their unresolved emotional issues with parents, siblings, and other family members by reducing or totally cutting off emotional contact with them. This is an attempt to reduce the anxiety or tension in a familial relationship through distance, be that emotional or geographic. In the end, this approach actually resolves nothing and in fact risks overstating the importance of new relationships.

8. Societal emotional process. This concept describes how the emotional system governs behavior on a societal level.

In summary, Bowen's Family Systems Theory attempts to explain the ways in which one is emotionally hinged to one's family of origin. It is a framework for understanding the complex and often invisible dynamics that occur within families.

From Theory to Practice

With Bowen's eight pillars providing a framework for understanding the complex and often invisible dynamics that occur within families, I began to develop my own comprehension of the primary drivers of emotional fluency in affluent families. In every instance, I look first to an individual's family of origin, meaning parents and siblings, for I agree with Bowen that the nuclear family provides the most intense set of emotional relationships you will ever have. *You are more emotionally hinged to your parents and siblings than you will ever be to another person in your life, even your own spouse and children.* This does not mean that you love them more; it just means you are more emotionally reactive to them than you are to anyone else. This emotional intensity can create both wonderful and painful realities.

THE LIGHT BULB GOES OFF

When I first met the Reynolds family, a mother and her five adult children, they appeared good-natured, at ease with one another, bright and emotionally intelligent. I enjoyed our meetings and found an easy connection that assisted our work together. They had inherited a business from the father prior to his early death that had been subsequently sold, and the proceeds, many millions of dollars, needed investing, estate planning, and philanthropic decisions. I met with the matriarch and her sons and daughters as a group many times to make the first set of decisions about the allocation of trust assets.

After three days of meetings, however, they were still unable to make any decisions regarding the assets. Each night my colleagues and I would return to our hotel and rework the charts and graphs we were using to help them assess the risks and opportunities of the various allocations to U.S. equities, bonds, hedge funds, international equities, real estate, and private equity. And each day they would balk. Eventually I began to realize that their inability to reach consensus had nothing to do with the actual content of the decision and everything to do with the relationships around the table. It was a thunderbolt moment for me. It also began, for them, an exploration of the emotional undercurrents that were moving their family on a constant basis. The mother and her children turned out to be highly emotionally intelligent, curious, and willing to work hard to improve their relationships and have found over many years that they have a strong and resilient bond that can withstand much.

This meeting was the impetus for me to study Family Systems Theory and explore the human dynamic of family. What I learned was that the impact of familial relationships on each individual was much more powerful than I had ever understood. I learned that our ability to function well in our family of origin is challenging, and that wealth makes it even more so. When one has ongoing "business" with their parents and siblings, the relational complexity is greatly increased.

When a family has financial wealth and abundance, emotional complexity is often heightened. Most families don't have a constant, sustained need to make a wide variety of decisions together in the same way that families with joint enterprise and business interests

"*Look, if we never went to bed angry we'd never sleep.*"

must. The average family makes group decisions around holiday plans, aging parents, and vacation and family rituals. Wealthy families must make these and hundreds of other decisions together each year, from estate planning to philanthropy, next-generation issues, and strategic business or enterprise decisions. To be successful, they must learn to minimize the adverse emotional content of these decisions—the emotional undertow—that can sabotage good decision making and eventually mire the family in failure.

Achieving emotional fluency requires courage and persistence. Without it, the emotional baggage of the family can undercut even the most intelligent and well-conceived structural supports.

Here's an example of an unfortunate outcome.

Many years ago, a family I knew was seeking an investment firm to manage the vast fortune they had accumulated. The eighty-plus-year-old mother, her one son, and her three daughters asked if I would help them reach consensus on which firm to join.

I declined due to the personal relationship I had with one of the daughters, but offered to help find them a facilitator. I did my due diligence and found a highly acclaimed lawyer/facilitator/author/lecturer who was also a well-regarded family counselor. I checked his references, spoke to clients, and even had him facilitate a meeting with my own family as a further screening element. He seemed terrific. He followed standard practice by interviewing the family members individually by phone in advance, and then arranged a meeting for the whole family.

Within fifteen minutes of his opening remarks, however, bedlam had broken out. The mother had gone so far as to sneer at one of her daughters and say, "I have always hated you." After ten minutes of tears and shouting, everyone stood up and left, leaving the facilitator alone at the table. It was a terrible moment for him and an embarrassment and deep regret for me. He couldn't manage the highly charged nature of that family and he missed the signs that may have been present in his phone interviews. Further, his very presence as a neutral voice in some ways gave the family members the courage to verbalize the emotional feelings they had long buried.

No one in that family was focused on the part they themselves were playing in the difficulty; they were only able to focus on their own pain and their deep emotional hurt and anger at the others in the room. Without understanding these complexities, there is little hope for repair and renewal. Such long-held hurts and close-to-the-surface pain only emphasizes the need for a highly skilled facilitator.

What could have been done to avoid this? Perhaps little at this late stage in the decades-long family pain. Another facilitator might have picked up clues in his phone interviews, but it's hard to say. To be sure, it was important to have a facilitator there, and many a family has avoided eruptions with a neutral, experienced facilitator running the meeting. But I tell this story to illustrate the dynamic, complex nature of family meetings, the ways in which pain and hurt can surface unexpectedly, and the crucial nature of emotional work in families.

The Role of Trust

As I work with multigenerational families, I often deal with the issue of trust. There is the matter of whom is trusted, how much they're trusted, and the various forms of trusts they must put in place to manage their affairs. The word "trust" is almost as ubiquitous as "values"! Priscilla Friesen and Kathy Wiseman, of the Learning Space in Washington, D.C., have helped me understand the connection between trust within a family and the development of self in that family. Both

Friesen and Wiseman worked for many years directly with Dr. Bowen. When Bowen described being a "self," he meant being able to take responsibility for one's own self, being able to observe the part one plays in a family situation, holding steady in the face of family conflict, and staying connected no matter what. Too often we attribute the notion of trust outward, with the responsibility for trust sitting squarely on the other instead of on one's own self. This is a mistake.

> *Trust has come to mean focusing on what we expect, need, or want from another. When expectations are not met, when we see things differently from others, or when we lose confidence in the behavior of others, we react. When intensity increases, our automatic response is to pull away emotionally and move toward cutoff. Cutoff is a process of managing unsolved emotional issues with parents, siblings, spouses, friends, and business associates by reducing or totally cutting off genuine contact with them. This resolves nothing.*[10]

Emotional cutoff is observed in virtually all humans and in many other species. Simply stated, we close down and move away, in one form or another, from those who are causing us discomfort or pain. We are hypervigilant to the anger, judgments, and rejections—real or perceived—of our family members. We are much more sensitive to the anger, judgments, and rejections of those inside our family than to those outside of our family of origin. To put it simply, because of this hypersensitivity and accompanying defensiveness, it's hard to nurture trust. As I've said earlier, in order to develop and nurture trust, one must be willing to be vulnerable, a tall order when we are supersensitive. Additionally, we must forgo the long-held reflex to blame others and instead look within ourselves for the part we play in the dance of mistrust. This very important work, that of examining our own contribution to the emotional complexity in our family, takes time and patience.

Too often I am called by families who want me to facilitate a program on trust and communication in hopes that the skills learned and insights gained will repair the strained relationships and frayed levels of trust their family is experiencing. I can help them identify the issues and patterns, but it takes more than a daylong program to facilitate real, sustained change. It takes time and commitment to stay in relationships, pushing through the urge to run away or blame the other and attending instead to the relationship itself. It takes some optimism on the part of the family, a resolute belief that indeed they can improve the relationships and ultimately become closer. And it almost always takes the help of a facilitator, consultant, coach, therapist, or advisor to shepherd the family through the work responsibly and sensitively.

Below, Wiseman describes what she thinks contributes to sustained change and improved familial relationships.[11]

1. Observe. Closely observing oneself in repeated interactions can lead to a deeper understanding of the nuances of one's own behaviors/views and those of others. Each interaction has at least two sets of perceptions. It takes practice to continually observe oneself and others in context. It is in the repeated observing of interactions between people that learning and integration of new ideas takes place. This learning is partly about seeing the difference between what we perceive in the actions of others and what the other intends. Observing and reflecting on our own actions and communicating about them thoughtfully are a part of the ongoing process that reforms the basis for trust in self. (By trust in self, I mean the confidence we have that our reactions to others are real and authentic, not driven by fear, hurt, or pain.)

2. Repeat interactions. Overcoming reactivity based on past experience is a process of engaging repeatedly. When people begin with a commitment to take the next step toward a deeper understanding of others, despite frustration, a greater level of engagement is activated. It takes special effort and purpose to move into an interaction with another with whom you have a relationship that has had past problems. Somehow one must learn to lean into the sensitivity. What develops is the capacity to interact with the other without fear of being harmed. One is building trust in self to manage one part of the relationship. A lack of confidence in others' thinking or actions initiates automatic distrust. This is exacerbated by a lack of confidence in one's own thinking or core strength. Initially there will be little focus on building trust directly.

With a history of more failures than successes, it takes perseverance to overcome past habits of interacting. The challenge is that only through a willingness to re-enter the overly sensitized, untrusting arena and begin interacting again can that trust be rebuilt. Think of trust as a muscle that can be made more powerful only through repetition; think of it as building strength through enduring stress. The challenge is to stay in your seat, listen carefully, and work toward understanding, even when your very cells say, "Why bother?" or "I'm out of here." After a perceived untrusting experience or a lifetime of eroding trust in a relationship, the challenge is to commit to a continued process that 1) shifts the focus to oneself and 2) reconsiders labeling the other as untrustworthy. These abilities form the basis for managing oneself and being sensitive to others. It is from thoughtful self-management that we can develop long-lasting, trusting relationships. The challenge is in the doing.

Common Hurdles

1. PRODUCTIVE NARCISSISTS. Author, psychoanalyst, and anthropologist Michael Maccoby describes the emotional issues that often envelop a very successful individual and block that person from achieving emotional fluency as "productive narcissism."

The Productive Narcissist, according to Maccoby, is an individual whose gifts and goals have created enormous success for many. These tremendously successful individuals have amassed great wealth, power, and fame as they have built their businesses, often from the ground up, into shining examples of corporate profitability, and they have done so on the wings of their own narcissism. (Maccoby cites Jack Welch, Oprah Winfrey, Martha Stewart, and Bill Gates as high-profile Productive Narcissists.) The challenge they face is that the very skills that brought them corporate success may stand in the way of their achieving emotional fluency. The Productive Narcissist is often a tireless workaholic, a passionate visionary, and utterly unshakable from attaining his or her goals. Productive Narcissists are consumed by their own vision and the rightness of it. That's all good if you're building a business, but problematic when you're a family member asking for a compromise or being asked simply to be at home for dinner once in a while. The Productive Narcissist is able to succeed in a chosen professional field, but has tremendous difficulty "turning it off" for family time.

This inability to stop achieving can actually create difficulties for the business. Consider the issue of succession. Can the Productive Narcissist step back enough to let others learn the ropes of leadership? Can this driven, passionate, single-minded individual demonstrate enough flexibility to let others lead once in a while? Can they give credit to others for their contributions to the business? Can they see and share their own weaknesses and vulnerabilities with their family? Often the answer is no. This is how the Productive Narcissist's emotional issues can rise up and create trouble.

But this situation isn't totally hopeless. As Maccoby explains, the key is to temper the narcissistic tendencies of the company leader with a substantial helping of strategic thinking. A good strategist will be able to see beyond his or her own emotional wants and needs and understand that for the overall good of the firm (and the family!), personal impulses must sometimes be, well, "squelched." It's a big leap for some, but not impossible, particularly when said leader has sought outside consultation or guidance. When given a process to harness those emotional impulses for good, it's sometimes possible to guide the Productive Narcissist forward to emotional fluency.

2. THE HERO'S FAREWELL. Professor Jeffrey Sonnenfeld of Emory University describes another challenge to emotional fluency, this one stemming from an event rather than a personality type.[12] What often emerges when a respected, powerful leader steps down is an unleashing of a torrent of related emotional responses that block emotional fluency, not just in the company founder but throughout the structure of the family.

For many in a family business, the title of "hero" for the founder and leader is not an overstatement. Often, that person really is a hero to the family—revered, respected, even worshipped. When that person leaves, others in the family structure may panic. This is the individual who created wealth and security for years. What will become of the family now?

At the same time, the hero may encounter unexpected emotional issues within, finding it much harder to leave than expected. I've seen situations where a "retired" leader still comes into the office, still hovers over the people named as successors, can't seem to let go of the reins of the firm, even undermining the new leader's authority and decisions. This is understandable but, frankly, dangerous. A hero who has said farewell but can't or won't follow through undermines both the financial stability and the emotional fluency of the family. The mixed signals of the lingering hero are quite threatening.

The solution for this particular issue is preparation. The most successful farewells I've seen are the ones where the hero moves on to a new challenge—running a nonprofit, for example, or diving into some other passion. Simply trying to sit back and relax is generally a recipe for disaster. This is an individual who thrives on doing, solving, conquering, and creating. Heroes need to prepare for their farewell by preparing for their next challenges. Without a challenge, they may be tempted to meddle in the leadership efforts of the company that's left behind. That's emotionally problematic for everyone involved.

The hero isn't the only one who needs to prepare. The next generation must also participate in this process, making the emotional transition from following the older, wiser leader to whatever the new configuration of leadership may be. Perhaps one sibling or family member will rise to the hero's position. Or an outsider may join the firm in this role. Whatever the new configuration, it will represent change. And the best way to ensure a smooth change is to discuss it extensively in advance—airing emotional issues that may be blocking a fluent relationship from going forward.

3. SIBLING RIVALRY. What can be better than the deep and devoted connection among siblings? Plenty! Just because you happen to have the same parents doesn't mean you're alike in any fundamental ways, or that you have similar styles, values, or priorities. And sibling relationships that include a business, accumulated wealth, or an enterprise of any sort to co-manage are all the more complex. The root cause of so many sibling conflicts or tensions? A fierce competition for the love of the parents (more on this shortly).

Another big issue to confront in the sibling relationship is the difference between "equal" and "fair," and when each of these constructs is most appropriate.

It's not uncommon for the highly charged issues of money and power and love to overlap when dealing with families of great wealth. The problem is that the solution to one is not always the solution for all. Take love, for example. There should never be a question of who Mom or Dad loves best. Love should be handed out freely and equally among all siblings. Not so when it comes to power or money.

My advice is this: when it comes to money, families can't always treat siblings equally, but they can and should always treat them fairly.

In one family I know, the terms of the inheritance differ between two siblings. One, an individual who has struggled with a variety of emotional problems, has his money in a trust. His sister, who has not had those particular challenges, received her share outright, without the restrictions of a trust. This may not be equal, but it is certainly fair. The arrangement seeks to ensure that both siblings get what they need.

In another scenario, a successful father left his company to his four children. However, only one of the four worked in the business (the others chose different career paths). Should all four be equally compensated? Is it appropriate that one sibling should have more effective power than the rest? Again, I go back to the difference between equal and fair. Splitting the firm into four equal parts might seem easy, but it's perhaps less fair to the individual who put the most sweat equity into making the company successful going forward. Instead of equally, the firm might be divided in a way that is fair. And the one running the company should indeed have more power in making business decisions than those not involved in the day-to-day business. If that new leader is wise, he or she will overcommunicate, seeking meaningful input from the others and working hard at those relationships.

Often, families are afraid to face the concept of fair and so fall back on equal. Perhaps it seems easier, less fraught with problems. But while equal may provide quick initial resolution, it often creates problems down the road. If all is equal but not fair, sooner or later resentment will build and corrode the family bonds. The "equal" solution is often a key barrier to emotional fluency. Many in the family may feel it is unfair and their resentment may leak out in other family interactions—not just in the office. Fair is messier, but often it is the most appropriate, equitable, long-term, and positive solution.

4. THE CHALLENGE OF SPOUSES. A large trust company once asked me to facilitate a discussion among the spouses of their wealthiest clients. The group, about twenty-five men and women, were seated around a conference room table. I opened the discussion by asking everyone to tell the group why they had chosen to come. The young woman to my left began, opening her mouth to speak and then bursting into tears. She said nothing else for the next ninety minutes. As we went around the table, each person spoke of the complexity of their role as spouse. They spoke of fear and longing, of embarrassment and of responsibility. They all acknowledged the tremendous opportunity and security they felt, and then dove down into the emotions they had that were perhaps less easily explained to friends or family. In this group of peers, however, they could talk about the price they felt they paid for the life they were living. It was a rich and spirited discussion that went on for two hours. The participants found in one another a group of peers, with similar experiences and feelings.

One common challenge that they discussed is based on pure socio-economics. Spouses who were not born into wealth bring different experiences, history, and diversity to the family. What they don't bring, however, is vast experience on how to be wealthy. This can be hard. They often feel judged by the community, and pressured by the family to perform in a particular way and be a particular kind of person. They often lack a kind of daily social fluency with the norms and actions of the wealthy.

This point is illustrated in a story told to me by a client recalling an experience she had in the early months of courtship while dating a man from one of America's wealthiest families. On her first weekend visit to his parents' home they gathered in the large, ornate dining room for breakfast and the butler asked her what she would like to eat. She replied politely, "What are you serving?" He seemed confused. He repeated the question and she repeated her answer, though she was beginning to realize that she might be making a mistake. He stood there, waiting. She was now paralyzed. Her boyfriend was no help. His mother stared at her. After what seemed like an eternity, the butler offered, "Perhaps some eggs, Miss?" She was saved. "Yes! Eggs!! Perfect," she blathered. Ugh. In her house they ate what her mom served; they didn't put in orders for what they wanted. Then again, her family of origin didn't have cooks and butlers.

I once heard someone say they had no idea that "summer" was a verb, as in, "Where do you summer?" (A wealthy friend's mother had asked her where she and her family summered and she was flummoxed.) These are simple examples of the ways in which maneuvering a wealthy life can be challenging for a spouse. Both stories tell of feeling unsure of oneself within new norms, rituals, and language.

Once married into a wealthy family, there are myriad complexities and new rules to understand. Something as simple as sharing the details of one's life with your non-wealthy siblings can become a minefield. So much information can't be shared, and then there's the information you're simply uncomfortable sharing. When siblings or parents are in very different financial and social circumstances, it often becomes deeply difficult to share the details of your life with your family of origin. And these "secrets" promote distance and separation.

5. TRUSTEES AND BENEFICIARIES. The emotional relationship between trustee and beneficiary is one that not everyone thinks of as a bond that should be tended to, yet it is a key element in long-term emotional fluency and overall happiness.

The beneficiary doesn't typically choose the trustee. He or she may be quite unhappy that there even is a trustee. If this is the case, then it behooves you to find a way to make this relationship work because, frankly, the trustee is obligated to his or her appointed role. The marriage, so to speak, has been arranged. The question is: how can it best be managed?

- Too often trustee/beneficiary relationships are conducted via paperwork. Take the time to meet, exchange views, discuss goals. This can be the foundation for a fruitful and emotionally satisfying relationship.

- Both the trustee and beneficiary need to invest time and energy in the relationship. A once- or twice-annual hour-long discussion of investment performance, distributions, and potential upcoming withdrawals is not enough. Sharing dreams and opportunities, as well as areas in which the trustee can potentially be helpful, are wise steps to take in building this important relationship.

- I've seen many cases in which the beneficiary doesn't treat the trustee with respect—doesn't show up to meetings on time, fails to treat the individual as a professional. At the same time, I've seen trustees who treat the beneficiaries as flighty or irresponsible. Both parties need to show respect and appreciation. You're all in this together and the relationship has the potential to be satisfying and rewarding for both, but that won't happen without attention.

Emotional Fluency: Whose Challenge?

Who in the family typically has the most trouble facing and coping with issues of emotional fluency? If you guessed the patriarch, you may be surprised.

In a number of families I've worked with in which the husband has created the fortune, the mothers of adult children have seemed most resistant to work that family members are undertaking on communication, trust, and family dynamics. I've come to think that their reluctance is perhaps quite understandable.

In the most basic stereotype, the father was busy for many years of the marriage, building a fortune and providing substantial security. He was often away and distracted by the complexity of the business and his responsibilities. The mother's job was "simple": raise great kids. When those kids stumble, or external advisors suggest that the family would benefit from some enhanced communication skills, the mother can feel implicitly criticized and incompetent. She compares her job of raising good kids to the seemingly Herculean job of creating a fortune, and the implication is that she somehow came up short. Her internal voice exacerbates the misperception. All you had to do is what millions of parents all over the world do every day and you had resources to do it with. How could you have let this happen? Why would she want a family meeting in which everyone talks about how the family could flourish? We're just fine, thank you very much!

A very real complexity for the mothers in wealthy families is that they can easily feel invisible in the family story of success. The narrative of the wealth creation and creative, entrepreneurial genius does not normally include the mother, other than perhaps in a "woman behind the man" kind of way. She is absent from this defining family history. She frequently feels invisible.

These matriarchs, understandably, sometimes feel as if the attention the family receives as a function of the business or the family wealth simply provides a broader audience for her parental failings. She feels judged and observed by others in the community in ways that less visible parents do not. This pressure and tension can cause fissures in the marriage. Further, the husband can often be unavailable as a real partner in parenting due to pressures in the business, a delegation of duties that extracts a huge marital toll. Mom feels, right or wrong, that Dad points to her when the children falter. That's not to say that fathers don't point fingers—they can and do. But mothers feel tremendous pressure to parent well, to make up for the time and attention children often don't get from their fathers. They often wish to excel at parenting the way their husbands excel at their work.

Kelin Gersick, Ph.D., an experienced and skilled advisor to families and family businesses, says,

> *To the extent that a woman accepted the traditional division of la-*
> *bor with her executive husband, and made home and children her*
> *life's work, any outcome short of the ideal may feel not only like a*
> *reproach, but also as evidence that her dreams were too narrow to*
> *begin with. All families are imperfect, and all children have short-*
> *comings. If her children's happiness and accomplishments are her*
> *triumph, and their troubles her fault, it is no wonder that she feels*
> *bitterness and resists the intrusion of outsiders who now want to*
> *help "improve" the family.*
>
> *There is no simple intervention that can address this kind of disap-*
> *pointment and resentment. The children are moving on with their*
> *own young-adult lives, and it is not their responsibility to reassure*
> *or redeem their parents. The most promising opportunity may be to*
> *encourage couples to renegotiate their approach to parenting, and*
> *it is never too late for that. Figuring out how to parent adult children,*
> *and eventually grandchildren, may respond to her husband's post-*
> *midlife regrets as well as her own.*[13]

Another further complicated dynamic in highly successful families is that of a very distracted, busy father and an emotionally distant mother. If, for whatever reasons, the mother creates and sustains emotional distance from her children, they often struggle with intimacy and seek nurturing and safety elsewhere.

Alternatively, when the family wealth comes from the labors or family of the matriarch, the husband/father can feel diminished, marginalized, or powerless. A man who does not contribute a significant share of the family support often lacks a social peer group with whom he shares this unique position. Our society knows better how to relate to a woman who is supported by her husband's money than the opposite dynamic.

The role of the matriarch in family systems can be problematic, even after she's passed on. It's often said that when the father/entrepreneur dies, the family grieves but then finds ways to move ahead. When the mother dies, however, the family is in real danger of coming apart. The mother is so often the glue that holds the family together. She's typically the one to whom the children most relate. When she's no longer around, her children can feel freer to play out old, deep hurts with their siblings, thinning the connective tissue that binds them to one another.

Emotional Fluency: Whose Job?

Naturally, everyone in a family must work to promote a happy family life. But when it comes to crafting emotional fluency in a family of means, sometimes this requires leadership from a surprising place: G2 and G3.

In previous chapters, we've done a bit of exploration into the personality types of a wealth creator. Often, these are individuals of substantial drive and personal power. They are entrepreneurial and individualistic by nature, and success has only cemented their view that they are proceeding in the "right" way. But is it reasonable to assume this individual will look for ways to change his or her emotional ways? Not really.

As a result, the job of fostering and maintaining emotional fluency often falls to the next generations. G2 and G3 may have the benefit of distance from the initial wealth-building process. They may be better able to step back from the demands of the business to see how wealth building can and should fit into the emotional lives of family members. If financial success was fostered and led by G1, this next phase may require a new set of standard bearers. If the family is to remain intact and thriving into the future, then these "human capitalists" often have to develop skills and strengths that they rarely learn from their parents. This is crucial work if the family is to avoid the "shirtsleeves to courtroom in three generations" fate that many families face, where the first generation makes a fortune, the next spends it (and ignores relationships), and the rest occupy their time suing one another.

Successful, wealthy families have the potential and the tools to create a dynamic, resilient family for generations to come, but I can't overstate the crucial role of the inheriting generations to the cultivation of that success. And a large part of that work involves the cultivation of joy.

You are more emotionally hinged to your parents
and siblings than you will ever be to another person in
your life, even your own spouse and children.

FIVE

CULTIVATE JOY

"Joy is prayer. Joy is strength. Joy is a net of love by which you can catch souls."
—MOTHER TERESA

Ignoring, shunning, or actively repressing the sweetness of success is all too easy to do when wrestling with the complexities and responsibilities of wealth creation and management. The high stakes of building and growing often overshadow the sheer joy to be found in the experience.

If too much of the family energy is focused on money and power and assets, there is little hope a family will thrive. Of course it's critical to run the business well, set a succession plan, and prepare for the next generation of leadership. But it's equally important to cultivate joy.

I've worked with many families in which the second generation has stepped in and taken on the leadership roles that the founders/parents have asked of them. They sit on boards, run divisions, and lead organizations, enterprises, and foundations. They devote tremendous amounts of time to the family interests. Many of them feel gratified and fulfilled by this work; some go so far as to say they are living their dreams.

Many, however, derive little joy from this experience. The unintended consequence is that their own children see and suffer from the unhappiness. They study the body language; they read the verbal and unspoken clues. They listen at the dinner table to the difficulties their parents describe in dealing with their elders, siblings, and cousins around the business. They sense the frustration and difficulty that the parent experiences. And they flee. The legacy of unhappiness passed to the third generation is often evidenced by their absenteeism. The vigor and passion they saw in their grandparents is absolutely nonexistent in their parents. As such, they seek lives that are unencumbered by the family enterprise.

The mission of joy is typically cast aside as other priorities crowd agendas. The culture surrounding the wealthy is too frequently heavy with duty and obligation, with a tone that goes well beyond seriousness. It's a culture of gravity. Families often forget that the multitude of decisions they must make are due to their success and to the almost unimaginable good fortune they have and that, for the most part, they're only trying to determine the best ways to sustain, grow, and give away their assets.

Perhaps this misstep stems from worry. The founding generation worries about the success of their business, the creation of the wealth, and about the impact of said wealth on the next generations. They worry about how to make this success have a greater positive impact on the world—often through philanthropy. G2 and G3 worry about their own performance in relation to their parents and grandparents. Am I good enough? Will I be the person who messes this up? Am I worthy of this gift? Will I let my parents down?

Younger generations also worry about raising their own children in the midst of such abundance. And they struggle with how to deal effectively with their siblings in regards to the enterprise issues they face. They try to figure out how to be good partners, great parents, dutiful children, functioning siblings, honorable citizens, and impactful philanthropists. It all feels like, and is, work! And while, yes, they have the means to make this work as enjoyable as possible, and they lead lovely lives, they still labor under the weight of duty and obligation.

Furthermore, these younger generations reside in a pervasively evaluative culture, where it's mighty difficult to feel real happiness. There simply isn't the space or peace for joy when family members are "dancing as fast as we can."

It is also difficult, if not impossible, to be joyful when one is afraid, and many wealthy family members are surprisingly fearful—of failure, of betrayal, of embarrassment, of rejection, of being poor, of being alone. To deal with this fear they create layers of protection that masquerade as aloofness, apathy, or superiority. "I'm too [busy, important, impressive, needed, influential] to be happy," they seem to say. How enervating this must be; how joyless this must feel!

A never-ending spiral of stewardship, duty, responsibility, obligation, and legacy can irretrievably sap the joy from a family over time. I actually see it as a downward spiral, devoid of joy.

Conventional wisdom is that if anyone can be happy, the wealthy should be able to be. However, as Harvard Professor Shawn Achor explains, the lens through which you see the world determines your reality. Only 10 percent of long-term happiness is based on the reality of what really happens to you; the other 90 percent is based on how your brain processes the external world. If you are stressed or focused on performance, the possibility of failing, the risks and responsibilities you have, it is more difficult to be in touch with what gives you joy, much less reach a state of happiness.

Research further shows that success does not precede happiness, but rather that happy people are better equipped to be successful. A happy brain releases more dopamine, and dopamine enables you to think more clearly and creatively, to act more decisively, and thus to be more successful than those mired in doubt, anxiety, or misery.

The challenge lies in the fact that in our outcome-oriented, evaluative world, we are constantly moving the goalposts of what we expect of ourselves to "succeed." We constantly are redefining what it means to be successful to the extent that success becomes, in fact, unachievable. Many might ask, "What's so bad about that?" It sounds like the entrepreneurial spirit driving toward success, right? Perhaps, but it is also the birthplace of stress and disappointment. It is how and why so many feel so unfulfilled. Our success is never enough and, therefore, we are never enough. And within this culture of über-striving and the constant shifting of the goalposts of success—within this culture of stress and disappointment—it is difficult if not impossible to feel the lightness of life and joys in the moment.

A complicated truth for many wealthy families is this paradox: the more you strive and seek joy, the more elusive it becomes. The quest for happiness and joy can't be evaluative, with constant assessments about whether you are joyous enough. You can't order joy to come into your home.

My experiences with many multigenerational, wealthy families is that some have found ways to invite joy into their homes and into their lives, and in the process, their families have flourished. Some of the ways these families have found their joy can be summarized as:

- Look for possibilities
- Invest in your kids' dreams—part 2
- Tame the perfectionist

- Release the storytellers
- Search for meaning

Look for Possibilities

The Art of Possibility, by Rosamund Stone Zander and Ben Zander, is a sort of ode to joy. The Zanders validate the importance of joy to leadership and sustainability. They speak to the attitudes that enliven business and enterprise, rather than the obligation that saps energy, as illustrated in the following story:

> A shoe factory sends two marketing scouts to a region
> of Africa to study the prospects for expanding business.
> One sends back a telegram saying,
>
> SITUATION HOPELESS STOP NO ONE WEARS SHOES
>
> The other writes back triumphantly,
>
> GLORIOUS BUSINESS OPPORTUNITY STOP THEY HAVE NO SHOES

Family enterprises can be much the same. If not careful, the family members and their attendant advisors and employees can embrace an attitude of über-responsibility and obligation.

Additionally, much of the strength of *The Art of Possibility* stems from a revelatory experience recounted by Ben Zander, the conductor of the Boston Philharmonic Orchestra. He describes his own transformation, which occurred when he realized that his power as the orchestra's conductor and leader was directly connected to how much "greatness" he was willing to grant others. As conductor, he is the one silent musician in the room, and he must inspire others if they are to succeed as a group. This expansive view of leadership is one that moves from a place of control to one of orchestrated (literally!) joy and inspiration. He asks himself what he can do to help his musicians soar, not what they can do to lift him up as their leader.

Families, too, can experience this kind of organizational transformation if their leaders are of a certain mind-set, the kind that asks: What are we here for? How can we be a force for greatness within this collection of individuals? How can I as the leader inspire and enliven those I'm leading? Where is the joy?

And how, then, can we cultivate joy *and* keep families intact and engaged around the wealth that's been amassed? The families I've seen accomplish this do several things:

1. Seek to know the true calling of every member of the family and find ways to celebrate those gifts. In one family, the artist son is asked if the image from one of his paintings can be used on the company brochure. In another, the stepdaughter, an ordained minister, leads the family in a prayer of gratitude at mealtime. In a third, the schoolteacher son is asked to help plan activities during the company retreat that will be engaging and enjoyable for the employees' children and grandchildren. In each case, the passions of the family members—passions that are not directly business related—are valued and celebrated. This makes individuals feel seen and appreciated for their unique talents, which serves to encourage them to continue to connect with the family. It is when we feel diminished or judged that we tend to flee.

2. Take time for real fun. For many affluent families, the majority of interactions are about business, board meetings, committee meetings, governance planning, succession planning, restructurings, recapitalizations, strategy planning, and next-generation planning. *Families who thrive counteract the centrifugal force created by the wealth and business with joy and fun.* Some form actual "Fun Committees," charged with making sure there is time and space for lightness and joy. They plan parties, outings, jokes, skits, and storytelling. They include all generations in the activities and strive to engage all in the joy. They are careful, however, to resist the temptation to make fun mandatory—the parties are optional and there is no "penalty" for missing an occasion.

3. Celebrate the small moments. Another reality of the lives of the affluent is that they are rife with headline moments—the sale of the company, the awards, the recognition, the BIG trips, the lavish parties, the groundbreakings. But real joy more frequently lives in intimate moments, the sweet and the tender, the delicate and the lovely. One danger, particularly in the second and third generations, is mistaking big for meaningful, losing the ability to notice and appreciate the smallest lovely moment. This is partly because they are crazy busy; partly because they are in an evaluative mind-set; partly because they may be afraid of failure, or betrayal; and partly because they mistake BIG for significant. Sarah Susanka writes about the freedom that comes from moving away from the chaos and over-commitment and "taking our finger off the fast-forward button": the art, she says, of doing less and experiencing more.

> The question is, what would happen if we stopped to consider the possibilities inherent in the word "enough"? It is a word we hear all too rarely in our daily lives and in our own thinking. "I have enough." How does that sound to you? . . . The opposite of enough is too much. And many of us today are at the point where we have too much already and don't need more. We don't need more adrenaline. We don't need more muscle tone. We don't need more goods to fill our houses. We don't need more text messages to make us feel alive. We can keep playing this game until the end, but it's just not satisfying anymore. . . . But the truth is that [the] fear of stopping is separating us from real meaningfulness—the objective of our misguided accumulation behavior. . . . If we don't let ourselves slow down . . . for a while, we will never see what is hidden below.[14]

What is "hidden below" is the possibility of finding real joy in the moment, and that moment is the birthplace of real aliveness and the meaning we seek.

MYSTERY TRIPS!

A large family I knew had a once-monthly Saturday "family day" called a Mystery Trip, or, when the kids were being funny, an MFO (Mandatory Family Outing). Each of their eleven children was in charge of planning and executing the Mystery Trip, ideally something they themselves liked to do that they thought would be fun—bowling, a trip to the lake, a movie, an amusement park, a zoo, you name it. They had a budget to manage and transportation to figure out (what with thirteen people in the family!), plus timing and meals. The family loved these trips and they became a vital part of the busy family's connectedness. As adults, ten of the eleven children became entrepreneurs, a fact I attribute to all of the logistics, planning, execution, and budgeting they became so good at.

Invest in Your Kids' Dreams—Part 2

As I mention in Chapter 2, lifting your children up is one of the most powerful acts you can do as a parent. Instead of shining the light on your own accomplishments, dreams, hobbies, and passion, shine the light on those of your children. It could be as simple as finding a space (the basement?) for the staging and exploration area of your kids' hobbies—if your child loves to design clothes, get a sewing machine, table, iron, and paper for patterns; if your child dreams of being an architect, fill a portion of the basement with LEGOs and blocks and bricks. More important, spend time in that basement working with your children, side by side. Parents who do so invest more than money in their kids' dreams; they invest themselves.

"If you bring joy and enthusiasm to everything you do, people will think you're crazy."

William Haefeli

Tame the Perfectionist

Families who "think small" are often able to overcome a hurdle so well described by sociologist Barry Schwartz in *The Paradox of Choice*. It seems, he explains, that the more choices you have, the more you expect perfection in the choice you ultimately make. And the more choices you have, the less satisfied you are with the ultimate choice and the more paralyzed you are in making that choice. Schwartz tells a funny story that illustrates these points. As a college professor, he gets to wear jeans to work. It had been many years since he had last bought any and he needed a new pair. His kids sent him to The Gap. He arrived and was quickly approached by a young salesperson who asked him what he needed. He told her "blue jeans" and gave her his waist size and length. She then began asking him a list of questions about the specifics of his jeans. It went something like this: "What color? Indigo, classic, stone wash, medium blue, black, black ink wash, rigid wash, zen wash, colored, faded . . . ? And what kind of fit? Classic, easy, loose, traditional, slim, dropped crotch, standard, straight leg, skinny cut, boot cut, flared . . . ?" Schwartz describes feeling utterly overwhelmed as he entered the dressing room laden with more than a dozen pairs of jeans. In the end, he left with none! He was paralyzed by the choices. He now expected not just a good pair, but the perfect pair of jeans.

Many wealthy individuals and families can relate to this dilemma. When you can go anywhere on vacation, eat anywhere, hire any advisor, attend any conference, you overthink it. Each and every experience must be wonderful. You expect nothing but the best and are frustrated and disappointed when your perception of perfection isn't met. A client once told me that he often arrived on vacation to a sensational, idyllic location only to feel as if they should have gone somewhere else, and if only they had, their vacation would have been so much better.

I sometimes encounter this in my work, when families expect the weekend retreats or workshops I facilitate to be perfect. Each session, each speaker, each meal, the hotel, the handouts, and the learning must be flawless, not just good or even terrific. I have often seen this point reinforced by the ways in which the family assesses the experience (the weekend concludes with a questionnaire that asks many detailed questions about how it was and how it could have been improved). Far fewer families take the time to comment on what went well, what they gained, what they left with that they didn't have when they arrived—a thought, idea, knowledge, connection, insight, or a meaningful conversation. Rarely do they acknowledge (much less celebrate) their accomplishments. Why? An evaluative mind-set is the enemy of joy.

When we focus so intently on what needs to be done that we ignore what needs to be felt, we're trading love for improvement. When we look to examine and critique everyone and everything rather than accept that our lives, like everyone else's, are filled with both good and disappointing elements, we never reach the final destination of a positive emotional experience. We miss out on the beauty when we seek to control tightly. This is particularly common in wealthy families in which the original wealth generator preaches the values of hard work, constant improvement, and singular focus over "wasting time" on frivolous pursuits. Such values may be what made the family wealthy in the first place, but they're not the values that will sustain the family going forward. Second and third generations must step up to laud *and* practice the additional values—the joyous values—of connection and acceptance and communication.

Release the Storytellers

Legacy is so much more than financial inheritance. It includes anything handed down from the past. Your family's legacy—and values—

are more powerfully conveyed by telling stories than through legal documents. Furthermore, storytelling fosters positive emotional connections.

"We tell stories to remind ourselves of who we are and to tell other people who we are," says Donald Davis in *Telling Your Own Stories.* "The basic function of storytelling is identity maintenance. . . .When a person or a community is more interested in *fortune seeking* than in identity maintenance—stories are left behind and storytelling dies." [15]

Long before the written word, people told stories. They were part of the life fabric of the whole community, the glue that held a society together, as essential as food and shelter. Stories enter our hearts by engaging our imagination. Stories enable us to pass down history and values, wisdom of the mind, and wisdom of the heart. When we tell our stories we are engaged in the act of discovering and creating meaning. Storytelling enriches the teller as well as the listener. Telling stories also provides an opportunity to see your own life more clearly in terms of what's most important to you, what your values are, and to live your life more fully according to and in alignment with these values.

When we tell our stories, we offer three invaluable gifts to the next generation:

1. A better understanding of who we are and the forces that shape the values we're trying to transmit. The person hearing the stories receives a more complete picture of the parent as person; the teller can be seen not only as a parent, but also as a child, entrepreneur, adventurer, a learner, someone who has struggled and is making his or her way. Stories offer a broader perspective to the next generation, grounding the storyteller and his or her values in a context.

2. An opportunity to explore who they are and how they want to form their own journey. When we hear a story, we imagine ourselves there, identify with the hero, and make connections to our own lives and experiences. In the quiet act of listening, members of the next generation can imagine their own stories projected onto the template of the parent's story. Personal stories offer them an opportunity to discover how they are similar or different or both, and ways they wish to emulate or diverge from their parent's journey.

3. The tools to continue passing on the family's legacy. By modeling the act of telling a story, we teach the next generation the importance of stories and legacy. Our children and grandchildren learn to value the family legacy and eventually how to tell the stories themselves. And so the family legacy is preserved and passed on through the generations.

Passing our legacy through our stories is not only a way to teach our values, it is also the essence of passing on a sense of self-worth and identity to subsequent generations. Stories help to ensure that future generations don't define themselves exclusively by financial assets. They provide a narrative and a context based on personal triumphs and challenges.

Search for Meaning

Individuals who seek a deeper meaning in their lives flourish, as do families who seek meaning. Virtually every family who thrives into the third, fourth, and even fifth generations is grounded in gratitude and reverence for something bigger than itself. My colleagues concur: a well-articulated, purpose-driven life, as well as a spiritual or religious life, seems to contribute to the overall health of the wealthy families they encounter. While well-defined purpose or spirituality can be, and often is, hinged to a specific religion—and it doesn't seem to matter what religion—I find that families who flourish see themselves as fortunate and deeply blessed, not as having been just smarter and more savvy than others. They have a practice of giving thanks, in whatever form it takes for them. They speak about gratitude to their kids and raise them accordingly. They have a construct for their lives that extends well beyond what they do, what they have, and even what they care about. It speaks to a deep meaning, a reason for their existence, and it is a compass by which they navigate life. They celebrate love in all its forms in their lives.

"Ultimately, what leads to wise choices is love—the attention to others as ends in themselves, as I am an end in myself, not a means to an end," says Paul Schervish, director of the Boston College Center on Wealth and Philanthropy. "The way love is implemented and practiced is care, which is attending to the true needs of others."[16]

Joy is, perhaps, the place at which flourishing families ultimately arrive and take up residence. It is the real treasure that all their hard work, devotion, and intentionality produces. It is not a frivolous distraction but the deepest of dreams. It is the bounty that sustains them and becomes their true legacy.

When we focus so intently on what needs
to be done that we ignore what needs to be felt,
we're trading love for improvement.

Conclusion

Throughout this book I have sought to discuss the realities so many dismiss—the relational, emotional, and life challenges that face families of great wealth. To be sure, these families have many assets that others might wish for themselves or even envy. But the challenges faced by the successful are human challenges, and the emotions they wrestle with are universal human emotions. All wealthy families know this one truth: money does not buy happiness, and it certainly does not ensure that a family will thrive. Wealth may take care of many of the physical needs, but their emotional needs must be tended by human hearts.

So I began this book with the story of my own family of origin and the pressure we felt in sustaining connection and joy in the aftermath of my brother's death. In hindsight, I see that some of us, not unlike the families I work with, fared better than others in the longer run—and those of us who did fare well, did many of the things that I have come to learn to be so helpful for wealthy families. We sought emotional fluency with the help of professionals; we were clear about what mattered most and aligned our lives with those values; we had the courage to take risks and make mistakes and then learn from them without heart-binding regrets; we valued the gift of each new day and found reasons to laugh hard, often, even when there was little that was funny. My father, whose heart was broken, chose to open up to life rather than create a thickened skin of protection around himself. And my sister Susie and I both created families of love and meaning.

I have seen so many families of wealth practice naturally what I have described here and I have witnessed the impact. Did they do everything right? No, not at all. But they did enough to overcome the downward spiral that the potent mixture of money and family can create. In many ways one could say that they practiced the core principles of the middle class—diligence, hard work, family, connection, and meaning. And that has created a wealth of possibilities for themselves and for many future generations.

I have been fortunate to be part of several learning communities over these many years and believe deeply that we learn best from others. I invite the reader to send me your experiences, what has worked for your family, lessons learned, and what has been challenging. I welcome the opportunity to learn from you. I can be reached at: Ellen@ellenmperry.com

I wish you and your family flourishing!

Strategies for Families to Flourish

If we were to synthesize many of the elements in the book into a few important strategies, they would be the following.

1. Connect.

2. Make rituals and keep them.

3. Choose schools in which your child is "known" and celebrated.

4. Listen to your children.

5. Repeat #4.

6. Develop skills around difficult conversations.

7. Minimize secrets in your family.

8. Consider family meetings if you don't already have them.

9. Devote yourself to being a great parent.

10. Stay home and do homework with your kids.

11. If your kids are older, invest yourself in knowing their dreams.

12. Let your children teach you something.

13. Shrink your shadow.

14. Find many ways to teach your kids about money and investing.

15. Take Mandatory Family Outings, or Mystery Trips.

16. Be sure your children have summer jobs.

17. Embrace all kinds of diversity.

18. Learn to be vulnerable.

19. Look first at *your role* in a difficult relationship.

20. Define fair versus equal in your family.

21. Identify the next generation of human capitalists in your family and encourage them every way you can.

22. Find ways to capture some joy when your family is together.

23. Tell stories.

24. Look for others in the family whom you can lift up.

25. Find ways to feel grateful.

Thought-Provoking Questions

As I have worked with families over the years I have learned that many are willing and eager to tackle the issues necessary for flourishing, and want to navigate their way to a vibrant, connected family. However, they don't know where to begin, who to ask for advice, how even to think clearly about the right questions to ask.

I hope for those who read this book that they will glean some ideas to get them started. Following is a synthesis of some of the core questions one might ask themselves and consider together:

- **What are our family's most obvious strengths and weaknesses? Could we productively build on our strengths and work as a family on shifting our weaknesses? If so, how?**

- **What are my most pressing challenges as a parent? What are my strengths?**

- **How could I be a more engaged and constructive family member?**

- **Who is asking the hard questions, the deeply challenging questions, that get to the root of the family issues? What kind of reception is that individual getting?**

- **Who in the family helps the family flourish? Who hinders our growth and development?**

- **What is going right in my family and how can we do more of that? Be as specific as possible.**

- **What are the unexplored opportunities for communication, emotional growth, and joy?**

- **Who can we enlist in the cause of our family's hope and happiness?**

NOTES

1. Edward M. Hallowell, M.D., *The Childhood Roots of Adult Happiness: Five Steps to Help Kids Create and Sustain Lifetime Joy* (New York: Ballantine Books, 2002).

2. National Longitudinal Study of Adolescent Health.

3. From personal correspondence with Ned Hallowell.

4. Robert Kegan, *In Over Our Heads: The Mental Demands of Modern Life* (Cambridge, MA: Harvard University Press).

5. James Hughes, *Family: The Compact Among Generations; Answers and Insights from a Lifetime of Helping Families Flourish* (New York: Bloomberg Press, 2007).

6. From personal correspondence with Dr. Crace.

7. Craig Kielburger, Marc Kielburger, and Shelley Page, *The World Needs Your Kid: Raising Children Who Care and Contribute* (Vancouver, BC: Greystone Books, 2010).

8. C. Brené Brown, *I Thought It Was Just Me (But It Isn't): Telling the Truth About Perfectionism, Inadequacy, and Power* (New York: Gotham Books, 2007).

9. Walter Toman, *Family Constellation: Its Effects on Personality and Social Behavior* (New York: Springer Publishing, 1993).

10. Kathy Wiseman, "Trust in Families: Another View," *The Learning Space* (blog), January 10, 2011, http://thelearningspacedc.com/pages/blog/140/trust-in-families_another-view.

11. Wiseman, "Trust in Families: Another View."

12. Jeffrey Sonnenfeld, *The Hero's Farewell: What Happens When CEOs Retire* (New York: Oxford University Press, 1988).

13. From personal correspondence with Kelin Gersick.

14. Sarah Susanka, *The Not So Big Life: Making Room for What Really Matters* (New York: Random House, 2008).

15. Donald Davis, *Telling Your Own Stories: A New Resource for Discovering and Creating Your Own Stories* (Little Rock, AR: August House, 1993).

16. From personal correspondence with Paul Schervish.

Recommended Reading

Brown, C. Brené. *I Thought It Was Just Me (But It Isn't): Telling the Truth About Perfectionism, Inadequacy, and Power.* New York: Gotham Books, 2007.

Collier, Charles. *Wealth in Families.* Cambridge, MA: Harvard University Press, 2001.

Davis, Donald. *Telling Your Own Stories: A New Resource for Discovering and Creating Your Own Stories.* Little Rock, AR: August House, 1993.

Gilbert, Roberta M., M.D. *The Eight Concepts of Bowen Theory: The New Way of Thinking About the Individual and the Group.* Falls Church, VA: Leading Systems Press, 2004.

Gilbert, Roberta M., M.D. *Connecting with Our Children: Guiding Principles for Parents in a Troubled World.* New York: John Wiley & Sons, 1999.

Godfrey, Joline. *Raising Financially Fit Kids.* Berkley, CA: Ten Speed Press, 2003.

Hallowell, Edward M., M.D. *The Childhood Roots of Adult Happiness: Five Steps to Help Kids Create and Sustain Lifetime Joy.* New York: Ballantine, 2002.

Hallowell, Edward M., M.D. *CrazyBusy: Overstretched, Overbooked, and About to Snap!* New York: Ballantine, 2007.

Hausner, Lee, and Douglas K. Freeman. *The Legacy Family: The Definitive Guide to Creating a Successful Multigenerational Family.* New York: Palgrave Macmillan, 2009.

142

Hughes, James E. Jr. *Family: The Compact Among Generations; Answers and Insights from a Lifetime of Helping Families Flourish.* New York: Bloomberg Press, 2007.

Hughes, James E. Jr. *Family Wealth: Keeping It in the Family; How Family Members and Their Advisers Preserve Human, Intellectual, and Financial Assets for Generations.* Princeton, NJ: Bloomberg Press, 2004.

Kegan, Robert. *In Over Our Heads: The Mental Demands of Modern Life.* Cambridge, MA: Harvard University Press, 1994.

Khan, Shamus Rahman. *Privilege: The Making of an Adolescent Elite at St. Paul's School.* Princeton, NJ: Princeton University Press, 2011.

Kielburger, Craig, Marc Kielburger, and Shelley Page. *The World Needs Your Kid: Raising Children Who Care and Contribute.* Vancouver, BC: Greystone Books, 2010.

Lansberg, Ivan. *Succeeding Generations: Realizing the Dream of Families in Business.* Boston: Harvard Business School Press, 1999.

Levine, Madeline, Ph.D. *The Price of Privilege: How Parental Pressure and Material Advantage Are Creating a Generation of Disconnected and Unhappy Kids.* New York: HarperCollins, 2006.

Mogel, Wendy, Ph.D. *The Blessings of a Skinned Knee: Using Jewish Teachings to Raise Self-Reliant Children.* New York: Penguin, 2001.

Mogel, Wendy, Ph.D. *Blessings of a B Minus: Using Jewish Teachings to Raise Resilient Teenagers.* New York: Scribner, 2010.

Morris, Richard, and Jayne Pearl. *Kids, Wealth, and Consequences: Ensuring a Responsible Financial Future for the Next Generation.* Hoboken, NJ: John Wiley & Sons, 2010.

Schuman, Amy, Stacy Stutz, and John L. Ward. *Family Business as Paradox.* New York: Palgrave Macmillan, 2010.

Schwartz, Barry. *The Paradox of Choice: Why More Is Less*. New York: Harper-Collins, 2004.

Siegel, Daniel, M.D., and Mary Hartzell, M.Ed. *Parenting from the Inside Out: How a Deeper Self-Understanding Can Help You Raise Children Who Thrive*. New York: Tarcher/Penguin, 2003.

Sonnenfeld, Jeffrey. *The Hero's Farewell: What Happens When CEOs Retire*. New York: Oxford University Press, 1988.

Susanka, Sarah. *The Not So Big Life: Making Room for What Really Matters*. New York: Random House, 2008.

Toman, Walter. *Family Constellation: Its Effects on Personality and Social Behavior*. New York: Springer Publishing, 1993.

Ward, John L. *Perpetuating the Family Business: 50 Lessons Learned from Long-Lasting, Successful Families in Business*. New York: Palgrave Macmillan, 2004.

Zander, Rosamund Stone, and Benjamin Zander. *The Art of Possibility: Transforming Professional and Personal Life*. Cambridge, MA: Harvard Business School Press, 2000.

Life Values Inventory. www.lifevaluesinventory.org

Spellbinders. www.spellbinders.org

Acknowledgments

*"We need to give each other the space
to grow, to be ourselves, to exercise
our diversity. We need to give each
other space so that we may both give
and receive such beautiful things as
ideas, openness, dignity, joy, healing,
and inclusion."*

—MAX DE PREE

I've had the enviable pleasure of learning from some wonderful
families and some of the country's most respected advisors and colleagues. Jay Hughes, a friend and mentor, changed the conversation
about families of wealth to the elements that matter. He and I have
had a deep friendship and collaboration and I, like many others, owe
him a debt that is inestimable. Additionally, he put his own family life
in my hands when he allowed me to arrange a date with a dear friend
of mine, Jackie Merrill, who now, twenty years later, is his wife.
She, too, has taught me life lessons about parenting, grandparenting,
and partnership. Ginny Rice and Wendee Wolfson are extraordinary
business partners. They have added immeasurably to the quality of
the work we've done and the fun we've had doing it. Our collaboration has deepened my understanding and capacity, fed my spirit,
and enriched my life. George Harris, Kelly Crace, Peter Evans, Anne
Hargrave, and Joe Judge are family advisors who are firmly rooted

in integrity, compassion, and depth and who have become dear friends and treasures. Kathy Wiseman, Priscilla Friesen, and Fredda Herz-Brown started me on a path in 1990, to understand family emotionality more deeply, and their collective and individual wisdom and exuberant generosity have added to my work and to my life. The families with whom they work are fortunate. Hap Perry and I began this exploration of family flourishing back in 1989 when we founded the firm now called GenSpring together, and I am grateful for a terrific ten-year collaboration that taught me much. There are indeed many others with whom I have collaborated and from whom I have learned, and I am indebted to each of them for holding meaningful conversations and asking profound questions that we all could grow from.

The families for whom I have worked are dear to me. I can't quite imagine my own family allowing a perfect stranger to enter our lives, fling open our kimonos, and expose our most intimate issues. Egads! What courage. Their stories are embedded in this book and in my heart. While some of them have graciously allowed me to tell their stories and share their journey, I have chosen to protect the identity of each of them within the individual stories and experiences I share in this book. I would be remiss, however, if I failed to say that you all are my teachers and I have grown immeasurably through knowing you. You have changed not just my life, but who I am. Your trust and generosity are humbling and I am forever grateful. Thank you.

The ideas and works of Parker Palmer, Dr. Murray Bowen, Charles Collier, Charlotte Beyer, John O'Neil, Rev. Alan Jones, Jay O'Callahan and Wendy Mogel, Paul Schervish, Ivan Lansberg, Kelin Gersick and John Ward, Dr. Kelly Crace, Dr. Edward J. Hallowell, The Collaboration for Families Flourishing, and Amy Fox have advanced the collective discourse we now all share and have been instrumental in my professional journey.

During this year of writing, several people have supported and encouraged me. Cynthia Wick, Paige Orloff, Margaret Lindenmaier, Amanda Close, Courtney Hundley, The More Than a Book Club, Deb Perry, Maria Nation, and Barbara Zhuetlin have been wonderful in every way. You all helped me to see myself as a writer and have held my hand through the frequent writer's blocks and crises of confidence. Thank you!

Rob, you have been my most gifted advisor, diligent editor, loving partner, and steadiest support.

Ellen Neuborne's skill was very helpful with the early manuscript. Perry Pidgeon Hooks arrived in the 4th quarter and became a wise coach, cheerleader, and enthusiastic supporter—thank you!

The extraordinary editing and design team of Lisa Zuniga, Tanya Fox, and Laura Beers were nothing short of magical. You were diligent, thoughtful, creative, and flexible. The book is dramatically better because of you. I cannot express the depth of my appreciation.

My husband, Rob Stein, is the love of my life and our daughter, Grace, is the beat of my heart. My stepchildren Gideon Stein, Noah Stein, Dorothy Stein, and Nate Perry have touched the deepest part of my heart and enveloped me with love, acceptance, and generosity. This book has each and every one of you all stitched through it. I love you.

Sit loosely in the saddle of life.

—ROBERT LOUIS STEVENSON